AN ARMY
ARISING

WHY ARTISTS ARE ON THE FRONTLINE
OF THE NEXT MOVE OF GOD

CHRIST JOHN OTTO

Belonging
House

An Army Arising: Why Artists are on the Frontline of the Next Move of God

Copyright (c)2013 by Christ John Otto. All rights reserved.

Published by Belonging House Creative.
visit www.belonginghouse.org

Designed by Zach Frey
Edited by Nancy Mari

ISBN-13: 978-0615906102
ISBN-10: 0615906109

TABLE OF CONTENTS

INTRODUCTION

PART 1: A CALL TO ARMS
11. A Moment in Time
19. A Secret Weapon
29. Know Your Enemy
39. Know Yourself

PART 2: BASIC TRAINING
51. Word Made Flesh
59. Crucified Artist
67. Living from the Inside Out
75. Sitting in Heaven
83. Holy People, Holy Things

PART 3: THE WEAPONS OF OUR WARFARE
93. Excellence
103. Saying Yes
109. Learning to Listen: The Voice of the Shepherd
121. Learning to Listen: The Creative Prophet
129. Living a Life of Worship
139. Rest
147. Taking Your Place at the Gate
155. Living for the Next Generation
165. Looking for a City

POSTSCRIPT

INTRODUCTION

I began writing this book in January 2013. I did have a sense of urgency about its completion, but it was the kind of urgency that every creative person has when they begin a new project.

On April 14, 2013 I found myself walking down Boylston Street in Boston. It was a busy Sunday and the streets were filled with excited visitors preparing for the Boston Marathon. That day a set of little mishaps forced me into the Back Bay neighborhood before leading worship at a new church in Cambridge.

Twenty four hours later two bombs would explode in Back Bay, killing three people and seriously injuring over 200 runners and spectators. Sadly, many of the runners finishing the race that day lost their legs.

As I wrestled with the aftermath of the bombings, and how close I came to my own death I was forced to rethink this book project. Two things became very clear. First, we are in a real war. It is a war of ideas, and there are people willing to kill for their beliefs. Second, if I died today, what is it that I would want to say? These two questions forced me to change both the direction of this book, and what I believe needs to be said to those who are called to fight in the Army Arising.

RAISE UP AN ARMY

In 2006 I experienced several months of extraordinary encounters with God that became the nucleus of my ministry, Belonging House. During that season I received a clear call from God to "raise up an army of artists to build Jesus a throne in the earth." For the past seven years I have prayed, pondered, and preached those words. This book is the result of this seven year process. I have attempted to distill in this book what I have learned about the call of God to the artist. I have also attempted to sort out how the artist fits into the picture God is painting right now at this time in history. About 5 years ago I wrote a book called *The Glory of A Wasted Life.* That first book was largely the story of how I came to grips with my own brokenness and the call God had on my life as an artist. At the time I didn't have the means to distribute the book before it was published. After publication, the last chapter and the postscript received the most feedback. The material about the call of the artist and how to embrace that call seemed to touch a nerve. This book is an expansion of the seminal ideas in those last few pages of *The Glory of a Wasted Life.*

AN EMERGING RENAISSANCE

In the past seven years there has been an emerging renaissance movement in the church. God is raising up arts ministries and artists in a new way. There have also been a number of great books written recently. I especially recommend *Unlocking the Heart of the Artist* by my friend Matt Tommey and *The Creative Call* by Janice Elsheimer. Both of these books deal with embracing the call to art, and learning how to release the gifts that are within. In beginning another writing project, I felt I needed to take a radically different approach from these two books. As a result, this book is about the big picture of what God is doing in the Army Arising.

It is also about the basic core of Christianity. From the conversations with the readers of my online drafts, it became clear that some basic Christian doctrine needed to be presented. Before I can talk to artists, I have to lay the foundations that sadly have been ignored for more than a generation in most of the Western Church. This prospect, though tragic, is also exciting. We are on the verge of a great awakening–and possibly a reformation–that will be global in scale. Unlike the writing of *The Glory of a Wasted Life* technology has allowed me the opportunity to build a conversation with readers. It was risky, but publishing the manuscript on Leanpub.com has proven to be a helpful process. Putting drafts out there "live" while you are forming ideas and writing chapters has proven to be a great experience. I am already grateful for the feedback I have received from friends. I am especially indebted to Nancy Mari who has diligently checked and rechecked the published text, caught errors, and even contributed to the tone and clarity of this work. I am also grateful to Salem Wesley United Methodist Church and their pastor Arthur and his wife Laura Savage. They have made a space for this work to happen. Thank you Maureen Smith and Martha Hart. Your prayers have been critical at several moments when I lost my way in the forest of words. I am also grateful to Jean-Marc Le Doux who helped raise funds for the project. I am also thankful to Zach Frey who designed the book, and the input and guidance of my dear friend Lyn Silarski.

Since returning to my "first love" of an artistic calling, I have had to face the pressure from other Christians to conform to other more accepted avenues of ministry. These pressures, both external and internal, have made me stronger and tested my resolve. I pray that this book gives you the strength to run after the high calling of the Army Arising.

Christ Otto
Salem, Massachusetts
2013

PART ONE

A CALL TO ARMS

CHAPTER ONE

A MOMENT IN TIME

I graduated from high school in 1989. As I was standing on the lawn in front of the school waiting for my family, my dad pulled on my sleeve and said: "Remember this day, because in 20 years you will look back and wonder what happened."

At the time, our world was still lingering in the Cold War mentality of the mid-Twentieth Century. The Soviet Union was still in power. The Berlin Wall was still standing. Islam was not perceived as a global terrorist threat. The controversies that would rock the Roman Catholic and Anglican churches were still fifteen years in the future. The Evangelical Church was still a cohesive whole in terms of theology and worship practice. Although the "worship wars" were beginning, most still considered the hymn and choir centered worship of mainstream Protestant churches the norm. The "Toronto Blessing" was still about 6 years in the future. A year before I graduated a guy named Mike Bickle made the news because of a curious band of "Kansas City Prophets" but the prayer movement his church would launch was still a small prayer meeting.

Along with this the technology of the Internet was still in its infancy. It would be a year before I first saw a computer connected to a telephone line. There was no email for the general public. The "Tech Bubble" hadn't happened. There were almost no laptops (they were big, heavy and hot). There were fewer cell phones and no smart phones. The iPad, and iPod for that matter, were still comic book fantasies. There was no Facebook, and "google" was yet to become a verb.

After college I entered seminary, and started to notice that things were changing.

In 1995 I was 23 years old and working for a center for preaching. One of the perks of that job was sitting in on Doctoral level lectures. One of those lectures is still burned into my memory. The speaker was Leonard Sweet, and he described himself as a "futurist." His lecture was like listening to a machine gun loaded with short shocking thoughts.

In the midst of this barrage he said one sentence that has stayed with me, and I have pondered again and again:

"The Church of the future is tribal, global, and post-denominational."

To describe a global church in 1995 was a mind-bender. It seemed (and was) practically impossible. A tribal church was novel, but also strange. There were glimmers of a post- denominational church, but they were far from an experiential reality.

It is nearly twenty years later, and much has happened, much has changed, and we live in a dramatically different world.
Another thing happened to me around that time. I was a very frustrated student, and I wrote this damning sentence in my notebook:

"These people are answering questions no one is asking."

Even at that young age I knew that something was off target. For the past twenty years I have watched as many in the Christian community continue to give answers to questions that no one is asking.

But many today are asking questions, and one thing I have observed in the past two decades is clear: The questions are being answered not by those who have the best answers, but by those who can most effectively use new technology to convince others their answer is the best. It's not the cake, but the frosting that wins the day.

WE ARE LIVING IN THE MOMENT OF THE STORY.

Whoever can tell their story in the most compelling way gets the air time, gets the attention, and sets the agenda. Never mind if the story is true, or even if the story is very good. What matters is that the story was told well. The best storytellers are the ones who can most effectively use the tools available in the most influential way possible.

For instance, I was sitting in a hotel lobby in Boston last week. In the lobby was the ever-present flatscreen TV with closed-captioning running at the bottom. The program was one of the dozens of daytime courtroom shows that fill the late afternoon. Since the sound was off, and I was sitting at a distance, I could really study the picture on the screen. I suddenly realized that the entire video image had been processed like a video game. The wrinkles of the judge had been removed. The entire image had been been edited. As I watched I noticed that the look of the defendant's face was slowly altered. As the evidence in the case was revealed, an editor changed the color and lighting on his face to look less attractive, and slightly menacing. At the same time the image of the plaintiff became equally bright and warm. The visual image was being intentionally distorted to influence reality for the viewer. I began to wonder what was real and what was a trick of the video editor.

This is an extraordinary moment, not unlike the day Gutenberg published his Bible. He did this the same year Columbus sailed to the New World, and within 25 years a dramatic shaking had occurred in Europe. Somewhere in the past 25 years we experienced a similar moment when civilizations, technology and culture all collided. We are living in the moment of interconnected, decentralized information. All of this powerful information is being transmitted through images and stories, not through words.

In seminary if I wanted to study the word "beautiful" in the Bible, I would have packed my bag with notecards and pencils, and headed to the library. Then I would spend hours finding commentaries, dictionaries, and concordances. The truth is, I would have learned some things, but my research would have only been as good as the books in my library, and I may have had to visit a second library to double check my sources. I may have never found some facts, like William Tyndale inventing the English word "beautiful." That fact would not have been in a Biblical reference book, but in an etymological dictionary.

Yesterday I spent 20 minutes during my morning study time doing the kind of research I described. I found all the information while drinking coffee, and I did it all while still sitting in my pajamas. Many do not grasp the dramatic shift that is happening all around us. Knowledge, and access to knowledge, is increasing every second.

Actually, there are many who do understand, and they are making use of this new power. There are leaders who are using the Internet, Computer Generated Image technology, video gaming, cinema, social networking, and personal technology to shape reality, ideas, and perceptions. In skilled hands trends, fashions, markets, and elections can all be manipulated seamlessly. Media is the water in the fishbowl. It determines the temperature, current, and food that impact us, the fish.

Nothing I have stated so far is new or unique. Many writers, Christian and non-Christian have made similar commentary. Some lament the shift, while others have seized it, hoping to form a new world. New questions are being asked, and many are attempting to answer them.

In order to understand this new world, we probably need to understand the story of how we arrived here.

In the first few centuries of Christianity there was a semblance of what we now call "five- fold ministry." Paul describes this in the book of Ephesians. Ideally, there are apostles, prophets, evangelists, pastors, and teachers functioning in the church to equip the whole community and bring them to maturity. For the first few centuries all the great saints who weren't described as martyrs were apostles. These were the brave men and women who went to new places and established the European church. These church builders converted Rome, the Mediterranean world, and Western Europe to Christianity. During this time if you wanted to go hard after God you went out to a new place and established a church. This was the age of Peter, Paul and, much later, Patrick.

The question being asked during this era was
"Who is Lord?"

The Empire said Caesar was Lord, and the Christians said "Jesus is Lord." Over time the Christian community converted the empire based on this ultimate truth. You can still see the influence of this first question in the basilica, originally a form of architecture from the imperial court. Catholic church vestments are based on the uniforms of Roman imperial officers. You can also see it in the dominant image of Jesus from this period—the judge enthroned in majesty looking down from the dome of the church building. The answer to this question worked as long as Roman civilization was functioning.

After Roman civilization collapsed, the Christian church was the only structure in society that remained intact. Things changed dramatically, and the church developed the monastic movement that was essentially a fortress of prayer in a hostile environment.

The monastery became the center of vital prayer, preservation of the Bible, and continuation of Roman culture. For the next six hundred years all the great saints were monks and nuns. It was this age that produced Francis, Bernard, and Clare. If you wanted to go after God, you entered a religious order.

**The question being asked during this time was
"Am I in communion with the Church
and do I know my place in society?"**

The answers to this question gave society order. Eventually this question would give the Western church tremendous power.

Five hundred years ago something abrupt and dramatic happened to the medieval order. The Protestant Reformers confronted the dominant church culture and the ignorance that fueled it. They challenged the monasticism that had been the center of Western Christianity for almost a thousand years. Both Luther and Calvin were shaped by monasticism and their reformation was a deeply personal response to their own experiences.

The question these first "modern" men asked was
"What must I do to be saved?"

Although the Reformation was necessary, the Reformers did not return us to the early church. They returned to the Bible as they understood it in light of the abuses of the late Middle Ages. Sometimes their decisions were reactions to the abuses rather than a real return to the early church. They only reformed as well as they were able in the time and place where they lived.

What the Reformers did was create a pastor centered church. And for five hundred years that church has served us fairly well. Since the reformation if you wanted to go after God, you became a pastor (or a missionary, who often was simply a pastor in another country). Even the Roman Catholic church eventually embraced this reality, and all the great saints in this era have been people doing some form of pastoral ministry–teaching, preaching, chaplaincy, and inviting you to make the decision to be saved.

Up until now all of these eras–the apostolic, monastic, and the pastoral–have all required someone to be professionally "religious." You had to be ordained, enter an order, or go to seminary to serve God. Now all of that is changing.

There are two new questions being asked today:
"Do I have value and where do I belong?"

At the same time, we are moving into a new moment when all of the parts of the Body are suddenly starting to function. Unlike before, you can now embrace a "vocation" to full time ministry and still do the craft you are gifted to do. It's no longer about church or denomination, its about kingdom.

This book is about this moment, and what it means. And I believe you are reading it because the Providence of God has placed it in your hands.

None of these shifts were a surprise to God. In fact, I believe that their timing, their unique development, and the quickening that is happening in time and space are all part of God's design. This is an important moment, and there is a triumphant reserve of men and women prepared for this time.

WHAT IS THIS MOMENT?

It is the moment of the story, and the storyteller. The one who overcomes in this moment is the one most gifted in telling a story. This is the moment of the artist. It is the moment of the troubadour, the dramatist, and the designer. It is the moment of the film maker, the novelist, the dancer, the puppeteer, the poet, and the painter. The storytellers have been set apart for this moment. If this is you, then this is your day, and this book is for you.

You are the one prepared to fight in a tribal, global, post-denominational army. You are uniquely equipped to answer the questions being asked today.

CHAPTER TWO

A SECRET WEAPON

In July of 2006 I had a dramatic encounter with God that changed my life. I was visited by an angel and I was told to "raise up an army of artists to build Jesus a throne in the earth." As you can imagine, after coming out of shock, I had many questions following this encounter.

"Why?" "What's a throne?" and, "Isn't gathering an army of artists like raising an army of feral cats?"

God knew that there would be a great battle between the forces of heaven and the forces of darkness some day in the future. We get hints at this battle throughout the Bible. Whenever God is going to do something, he leaves hints in the Bible. We call these hints "prophecy" and sometimes we don't see them clearly until right before we need them, and sometimes we don't see them until after the prophecy has been fulfilled. You can safely say that much of the New Testament is about interpreting the prophetic hints that led up to Jesus.

In the first chapter of the Old Testament book Zechariah we get one of these hints. It is a prophecy so obscure that many scholars have been unable to even agree on an adequate translation. The text isn't difficult, but the image it describes is hard to understand. Because of this, translators have stumbled on it. Even so it is there, and it is a vision of two armies.

This chapter is going to be an in-depth biblical word study. At moments it might be tedious, but press through. I am about to show you why being an artist is part of God's secret weapon. This study is the foundation for the rest of the book.

Zechariah chapter 1 ends with a vision of four horns that rise up in the earth to terrorize Judah, Israel and Jerusalem. In verse 20 the prophet then notices four smiths. He asks the angel in the vision what they are called to do. The angel replies "To throw into panic, to hew down the horns of the nations that raise a horn against Judah to toss it."

The Hebrew here is not clear, and even in most English translations the sentence is hard to understand. I came upon this in my morning readings, and out of curiosity hit the books to grasp the meaning. Most translation notes say the word "smith" was chosen based on the context of the sentence, but the context is not clear. We are not sure what the smiths are doing, other than striking terror into the horns that rise against Israel.

My curiosity increased, and I then went to the Hebrew to find the word translated "smith." Young's Literal Translation translates the word "artisan." Others translate it carpenters, engravers, craftsmen. Often the word makes direct reference to stonecutting and jewel work.

The root word is *charash,* and it appears 35 times in the Hebrew Bible. In all but two cases (33), the New Revised Standard Version translates it "artisan." The other time outside of Zechariah 1:20 is in Isaiah 41:12 where the prophet is clearly describing a blacksmith, so it is translated "blacksmith."

As I studied the use of the word in scripture, a clear picture began to emerge of how this word was used in other places. Especially important was the use of the word in the Five Books of Moses, the Torah.

The first use of *charash* refers to the two men who were anointed to build the Tabernacle, Oholiab and Bezalel. They first appear in Exodus 31. Exodus 31:3 is the first description of someone being "filled with the Holy Spirit" in the Bible. This is the only place in the Old Testament where that term is used. In Exodus 35:35 the men are described as *charashim,* "artisans." They are skilled in every kind of craft, from woodworking to weaving to jewelry making and metal work. We would call them "renaissance men." Their work looks like the workshop of a master from the Renaissance period, with jewels, tapestries, furniture, and costume all being fashioned under their leadership.

I would argue that these two men were the greatest prophets in the Old Testament. Under Moses' direction, they may have had encounters with the heavenly realm, and they must have heard descriptions of heaven from Moses. They depended on the Holy Spirit to make Moses' "courtyard of heaven" experience visible to the rest of Israel. Not only did their work become the access point for the people to meet with God, it became the origin of the holy imagination of the Jewish mind. They created the ark, the menorah, the cherubim, and the furnishings for the temple. These elements, and their design, are still fixed in the Judeo-Christian symbolic system.

As a side note, we will not meet another person "filled with the Spirit" until we encounter Mary. From this, we can draw a clear line between the artist and the Incarnation. **The artisan puts flesh on the work of the Spirit, and makes that reality visible for others to experience.**

Throughout the Bible the word charashim carries this understood meaning. The artisan is a renaissance person, able to do many things and create things of beauty. In the books of Kings and Chronicles, this term would be used to describe the men sent by Hiram to build the Temple (I Chronicles 14:1). These artisans do all kinds of work, just like Oholiab and Bezalel–carving, carpentry, stonecutting, weaving, jewel work, metalsmithing, and design. The Charashim are the artisans/craftsmen called to all kinds of workmanship.

Before looking at another important use of charashim in scripture, we should take a brief look at the contrast created in Exodus 32 between the artisan and the idol maker. There has been a tension within Christianity over these two roles for centuries. This tension became a symbol of the split between Catholics and Protestants.

GOD THE ARTISAN

God tells Moses he has called Oholiab and Bezalel to create the Tabernacle in Exodus 31. He is given a long description of what they are gifted to do. Immediately following, the LORD commands Moses concerning the importance of the Sabbath (Exodus 31:12-18), and He writes the two stone tablets of the Covenant (32:16). We should note two things in the context of this chapter. The calling of the artist is immediately followed by the extensive command to rest. Beauty and rest walk together. The next thing that happens is YHWH himself engraves the tablets of the Law. This is the first hint that we have of a direct link between the artisan and God. At this moment the LORD acts as the CHARASH, doing the work of a craftsman. We will see this more clearly at another place in scripture.

Already we are seeing the principle develop that part of the nature of God is to be an artisan whose work creates a bridge between the spiritual and natural realms. **In the same way, the nature of an artisan is also to create a bridge between the natural and spiritual realms.**

IDOLS AND ICONS

Meanwhile, because Moses has taken so long on the mountain, Aaron pacifies the people by fabricating a golden calf. It is an idol that he casts and they worship before it, just like the pagans. In these two chapters we begin to see the tension throughout scripture between the idol and the icon. An idol becomes a visual obstacle to God, a diversion from true faithfulness, and an excuse for immoral behavior. In the case of the golden calf we see drunkenness and debauchery as a result of their idolatry.

By contrast, the icon Oholiab and Bezalel created was a vehicle for engaging God, and also a means to live a life of holiness. Surprisingly, they were asked to create a number of things that might at first seem forbidden—cherubim, doves, oxen, almond trees, palm trees. These visual elements were intended to convey a reality beyond this earth using earthly imagery. Although there would always be an "iconoclastic" vein in Judeo-Christian tradition, it is clear that these images were a core part of the covenant with Moses.

To make this clear, an icon is a tool to use in worshiping God. An idol is an obstacle that demands worship in place of God.[1]

---

1 The Brazen Serpent in Numbers 21:4-9 is the best example of this icon/idol paradox. It was created for God to use as a vehicle for healing the people. It later became an idol, and King Hezekiah destroyed it (II Kings 18:4). Jesus later compared himself to the original use of the serpent when he linked it to the crucifixion in John 3:14-15.

To finally get a full understanding of the artisan, and what it might mean in Zechariah 1:20, we should look at a "throw-away" line from the genealogy in I Chronicles 4:14.

> *Meonothai became the father of Ophrah; and Seraiah became the father of Joab father of Ge-harashim, so-called because they were artisans.*

Here we see the word right in the translation, and we see that the name was given because Joab's descendants were artisans. In the footnote "Ge-Harashim" is translated "Valley of the Artisans." This verse is key because it shows that later usage of the word *charashim* was artisan, and this use was common at the time of Zechariah. This verse becomes an important key to understanding how this word gets translated into the Greek New Testament.

AN END-TIME ARMY OF ARTISANS

In Zechariah 1:18-21 we see four horns. The number four often represents the created order, or the earthly realm. Horns often represent government or military power. To make a leap using New Testament language, I believe we are seeing the world's powers rising up against Judah, Israel, and Jerusalem, and by extension those who have been grafted into the covenant with them. In response to the world power against God's people, there arises another four–four artisans. The image here is an army, an army of artists. What do these artisans do? They terrify the enemies of God, and this terror renders these world powers ineffective until they are struck down. What terrifies the enemies of God? A clear, brilliant representation of who God is and what heaven is like. These artisans are telling the story, and they are telling the story with force. And because the story is taking many forms–dance, music, visual art, cinema–it is difficult to stop or control. There is no argument against this onslaught of beauty. Zechariah is seeing an end-time army of renaissance men and women.

As I mentioned, I Chronicles 4:14 gives us a bridge to the New Testament. The New Testament writers used the Septuagint (the Greek translation of the Old Testament) as their Bible. The word used to translate *charashim* in Greek is *technitais*. You probably see the root of the English word "technology" or "technician" in that word. It is used only four times in the New Testament.

In Acts 19 we see Paul running into trouble when the silversmiths–the idol makers–in Ephesus cause a riot. These men are described as technitais. We also see artists and craftsmen in Revelation 18 listed among those who are judged in the final destruction of Babylon. These aren't God's end-time warrior artists; they are idolaters. Once again we are given the contrast between the artisan and the idolater.

Surprisingly, there is a final artisan mentioned in scripture. In Hebrews 11:10 we are shown the source of Abraham's faith:

For he looked forward to a city that has foundations, whose architect and builder is God.

The word "builder" in our English Bible is the root word *technitais*. God is the Artisan. He is the designer, and the master craftsman of the New Creation, and his final work is the creation of the Holy City, the New Jerusalem. Isn't it fitting that He would be preparing an army of artisans, expressing this unique aspect of His Personality, to begin making a way for the fulfillment of all things? God is bringing all things into order, and He is raising up an army to do it.

Earlier I mentioned that the charashim often are described as ones who work in precious stones. It is not surprising then, that Revelation 21 gives great detail about the giant precious stones used in the City–jasper, sapphire, emerald, agate, pearls, onyx, carnelian, and on and on. Not to mention all the gold. Jesus, who has gone to prepare a place for us, has been working as an artisan. And not only is Jesus working as an artisan; and he is also raising up the artisan. These ones who have seemed to have no value to the world system, are now being called as the end time secret weapon. That was the plan all the time, to astound the world with the sounds, sights, and smells of heaven. In the midst of great darkness, a new and glorious light will shine.

I guess it is no surprise that in places where radical Islam is taking hold that the arts are being made illegal. Islam has long forbidden artwork, but now there is an increasing intolerance to the great monuments of the past, to all forms of music and to any visual art. They are afraid of beauty, because beauty will lead us to the One who is beautiful. It is not a stretch to see that artists will strike terror in those who terrorize Judah, Israel and Jerusalem.

This is the moment for the artist to arise. This is the moment for the artist to make a way. This is the moment for the artist to be the sermon. Maybe this is the moment Paul spoke of in Romans 8:22 "All of creation is groaning for the revealing of the sons of God." This is the day for the artisan to be revealed and declare the glory of God.

TO RECAP:

- Zechariah 1:20 describes four powers rising up against God's people. In response, God raises up four smiths that strike terror in these powers and overcome them.
- The word translated "smith" in Zechariah 1:20 is usually translated "artisan" and is used to describe the artists who built the Tabernacle under Moses–Bezalel and Oholiab. Exodus 31 links the call of the artisan to the establishment of the Sabbath, and also sees God engrave the tablets of stone. This is contrasted with Exodus 32 when Aaron creates the golden calf. There is always a tension in scripture between the idol and icon.
- I Chronicles 4:14 shows us that "artisans" was the common understanding of "charashim" at the time of Zechariah, and also forms a bridge to the translation and use of the word in the Greek Septuagint and the New Testament word "technitais." God is described as the artisan (technitais) in Hebrews 11, and this reference is echoed in Revelation 19. Here heavy emphasis is placed on the jewels in the construction of the city, and jewel work and engraving are one of the special meanings of "artisan" throughout scripture.
- We can conclude that Zechariah 1:20 is referencing a new order of artisans that God will raise up at the end time battle of Jerusalem. This order is designed to strike fear in the enemies of Israel, and they represent a unique and intrinsic part of the character of God. Like Oholiab and Bezalel, they are called to make heaven visible. They are forerunners of the Holy City that God, the Master Artisan, is building.

CHAPTER THREE

KNOW YOUR ENEMY

So God is raising up an army of artists. In the last chapter the artist was described as God's "secret weapon" in his arsenal for this time. That kind of language is the language of war. If we are in a war, then we are facing danger. There will be casualties, and there is an enemy. And this enemy will stop at nothing to succeed.

This is no place for artists! So why would God use this kind of army?
The Chinese philosopher and military strategist Sun Tzu wrote in his book *The Art of War:*

"Know your enemy, know yourself, and you will not fear the outcome of a thousand battles." [2]

Before we explore the army of artists, we need to understand the nature of our enemy. It is important to understand the weapons in the enemy's arsenal, and why the artist is especially able to face the enemy.

A REAL WAR
St. Paul tells us in Ephesians 6:12 that we are not fighting a physical battle with conventional weapons. We are fighting an invisible war

---

2 Sun Tzu, *The Art of War.* Thomas Cleary, translator. Boston: Shambala, 2005. 15

in an unseen realm that may manifest in flesh and blood, but is not *with* flesh and blood. He describes our enemies as "principalities, powers, and rulers in spiritual places." In another place he describes not using worldly weapons and "taking every thought captive that exalts itself above our Lord Jesus Christ." (2 Corinthians 10:3-5)

For you who are from a charismatic tradition, you will be familiar with the term "spiritual warfare." This war is real, and it can have dramatic costs in our real lives. This battle of life and death is often very real in places where missionaries are taking new ground.

In 1993 the father of a dear friend was weeks away from finishing his translation of the New Testament. They were about to present the completed work to an unreached tribe in Papua New Guinea. Suddenly one morning his translation assistant brutally murdered him while they were working. After the crime was committed his killer awoke from a trance. Later it was recognized that he had been under the spell of a local witch doctor.

Just recently I was asked to pray for a mission team. Several late term miscarriages had occurred in the families of each team leader. At first they seemed like random tragedies until I began to notice the pattern in how they happened. It was clear that there was an occult assignment against this mission. It was also not surprising that the mission was in the heart of the arts community in a major European city. We face a real enemy wanting to rob, kill, and destroy.

Zechariah 1:9 describes four horns rising up to scatter Judah, Israel, and Jerusalem so that no man can lift his head. This is an image of a coordinated effort among various nations of the earth to oppress God's people.

Throughout the Bible, the horn is used as a symbol of power and authority. It is the symbol of strength and virility. In this case, the horn is the power to oppress. Zechariah sees four horns, and rather than trying to figure out who each horn represents, I believe the text is pointing to the symbolic nature of the number four. In the Bible four represents the four cardinal directions, this world, and the created order. In other words, the powers of this world in the nations are rising up to oppress Judah, Israel, and Jerusalem, and by extension, all those who are grafted into Covenant with God.

What is the power that is in the world that rises against us?
It is the Spirit of Anti-Christ.

I use the word spirit with caution, because some will say I am naming a demon and encouraging you to "cast it out." In this case I am referring to a larger thought system and its related power to influence leaders, nations, movements, and groups. These powers represent prominent forces at work in the world.

What is the Spirit of Anti-Christ? In the first letter of John chapter 4 we are given a very simple test:

> *Do not believe every spirit, but test the spirits to see whether they are of God; for many false prophets have gone out into the world. By this you know the spirit of God: every spirit that confesses that Jesus Christ has come in the flesh is of God, and every spirit that does not confess Jesus is not of God. This is the spirit of Anti-Christ...(I John 4:1-3b)*

There is a core truth that sets Christianity apart from every other world religion or belief system. To quote Eugene Peterson's *The Message,* "God became a man and moved into the neighborhood."[3] Any system or teaching that denies the incarnation is the spirit of Anti-Christ.

A SUBTLE ENEMY

In modern western culture we have a "spirituality du jour" and most of those spiritualities, although seemingly helpful or benign, often sidestep having an encounter with the living God in Jesus Christ. Any spiritual practice that denies that God came in the flesh does eventually agree with the spirit of Anti-Christ. As Pope Francis recently stated, "Whoever does not pray to the Lord prays to a demon."[4]

When we put it this way, suddenly a number of ideas, religious teachings, and seemingly benign groups come into sharp focus. Any idea or organization that denies that Jesus Christ is God in the flesh is a representative of the spirit of Anti-Christ.

The spirit of Anti-Christ takes multiple forms, but one has become evident in the United States. There has been a lot of pressure recently to rename Christmas or call it the "Winter Holiday." Public school children are not allowed to sing songs making reference to Christmas or the birth of Jesus. At times this pressure has taken a sinister tone. The core issue is denying the Incarnation of Jesus. If Jesus is not God in the flesh, he can be handled very differently, and his death on the cross, and even his resurrection can be reinterpreted, redefined, and re-imagined. More importantly, our

---

3 Peterson, Eugene, *The Message.* Colorado Springs, CO: NavPress, 2002. 16

4 "Pope Francis Warns Against 'Demonic Worldliness,'" March 16, 2013, CNSNews.com

response to Jesus suddenly changes as well. Often there is pressure to make Jesus irrelevant to our lives. Along with this, a personal God, who is a loving Father, can be replaced with a "universal life force" who places no demands on us regarding truth, relationship, or morality.

ANTI-SEMITISM

The spirit of Anti-Christ has taken many forms throughout the ages, but it always results in several things. Often it fuels the oppression and suffering of the Jewish people. God became a man, and the man he became was Jewish. In other words, God's DNA is Jewish. When Jesus shed his blood on the cross, that blood was Jewish blood, and that Jewish blood was spilt in Jerusalem, on Jewish soil. God's DNA is on the land in Israel, and whether they believe in him or not, Jews share this DNA with Jesus.

It is amazing how many times in history there has been a major attack on Jews that seem to correlate with moves of God in the earth. When Rome became Christian, there was a major persecution of Jews. The same thing happened at the time of the Reformation. A similar thing happened in Russia at the time of the Pentecostal outpouring. And of course, the nation of Israel was born after the fires of the Holocaust. As revival increases in the earth today there is a corresponding resurgence of anti-semitism and a senseless anti-Israel position in international politics.

THE SPIRIT OF THE AGE

Throughout history, the spirit of Anti-Christ also manifests in vain and deceptive philosophies that result in death. Often those most violently attacked have been children, babies, and the unborn. The German philosopher Georg Hegel coined the term *Zeitgeist* in the nineteenth century to describe a prevailing thought, intellectual fashion, or philosophy that dominates a culture for a particular period in time. Literally, Zeitgeist is translated "spirit of the age." The spirit of Anti-Christ can easily manifest in the spirit of a particular age. The French Revolution began as a revolt against real injustice in France, but ended with attacks on the church, the executions of thousands of nuns and priests, and a series of laws against Christianity that remain in force today.

Here in the United States the dominant philosophy at work is what I call Existential Darwinism. The Darwinism I speak of is quite a bit more nuanced than the "creationism vs. Darwinism" controversy. Existential Darwinism has made it's way into the core beliefs of most Westerners. The big question raised when we talk about Darwinism in this sense is not "how" God created, but why. I am not referring to the actual things Darwin wrote, but rather the consequences of his theories that have become a world view.

Here are some core tenets of Existential Darwinism:

1. Human beings have not been created for any particular purpose. They are not any different from any other animal on the planet, and in some ways, humans are actually inferior to other animals because humans have the ability to misuse the environment rather than live in harmony with it.

2. All animals are evolving, and over time are improving. This is usually called "natural selection." Natural selection is the strong overtaking the weak.

3. The process of "natural selection" should be encouraged. The strongest most adapted specimens of each generation succeed over weaker specimens in order to create a stronger species.

4. **Life and death decisions can be made based on the needs of the species, or the larger environment, regardless of their moral implications.** In fact, all morality is subservient to the animal instinct. This instinct is primarily driven by pleasure, procreation, and preservation.

WHAT EXISTENTIAL DARWINISM LOOKS LIKE

So for example, if you believe that you are the highest form of human beings that has evolved over time, you will believe that the beliefs of your contemporaries are more valuable than those of the past. Your educational system will focus on current issues rather than on the writings or knowledge of previous generations. You will believe that technological innovation equals moral superiority. What seems right and feels good is a strong enough reason to make a decision.

Because you believe that the strong survive, you will focus on physical strength over moral goodness. Sex will become the highest form of entertainment because it doubles as an indicator of physical strength. Because human beings are not more valuable than baby seals, abortion or infanticide is acceptable. Abortion serves a dual purpose because it helps control the population, and also allows for an individual's pursuit of personal pleasure. For that matter, any weaker member of society can be given a lesser value, and can be expended for the greater good. A society that embraces this philosophy begins to feel confident in choosing "winners and losers."

A church that embraces "E.D." believes faith enables you to find personal fulfillment, and the teachings of that church will often be adapted when the older, less "evolved" teachings conflict with the contemporary definition of core values. These values, because they are evolving over time, can change freely. Along with this, worship style and music can change or adapt at any time to meet the contemporary need over any received "style" from the past. This is because the current church has also attained the highest form of evolution over previous less highly evolved generations. **Process begins to equal progress.**

How this philosophy plays out in our daily lives is important. For the artist and the story teller, being aware of how much of this philosophy is informing your art is critical. It is what sets someone from God's army of artists apart from the other army. And because this philosophy is the prevailing one, even in the church, to challenge its tenets can bring a serious reaction.

DEATH IS THE GOAL

As you begin to understand the spirit of the age, you begin to understand how the spirit of Anti-Christ uses various forms of deception to achieve its ultimate goal: the death of as many human beings as possible who do not have faith in Christ. The spirit of Anti-Christ is working relentlessly to bring men and women to a Christless eternity in hell. The spirit of Anti-Christ wants to bring the ultimate destruction of humanity, which bears the image of God, in the most widespread way possible. This destruction is eternal separation from God and his goodness and love.

Whenever the spirit of Anti-Christ reigns, there will be unprecedented death and destruction. This is how we can explain the mass murders of millions of people in Nazi Germany, the Soviet Union, and Communist China. There was a committed effort to eliminate God, and especially any form of true Christianity from these societies. The end result was atrocities against humanity on an unprecedented scale.

The spirit of Anti-Christ uses two major tools to accomplish its goals: deception and fear.

Very rarely do we see deception come out in outright lies. Often the deception takes the form of subtle half truths repeated again and again. The media has been doing this for decades, by subtly inserting certain ideas into the story lines of programs. Hitler understood this, and almost from its beginning, the Nazi party began repeating the lie that Jews were responsible for the economic and social problems in German society. This theme was repeated in a thousand different ways, until finally the German people believed the lie as truth. Once the truth was accepted, the German people were comfortable with Hitler's "Final Solution" to the "Jewish Problem."

The second tool, fear, causes people to make poor decisions in life. Fear and panic will cause people to make bad financial decisions that take a lifetime to undo. For many years I worked in crisis pregnancy centers, and it was often said that "fear fuels the car that drives a woman to an abortion clinic." It has been very disturbing over the past several years to see how especially the news media will replay stories over and over again to cause people to live and act in fear.

When fear and deception work together, it becomes an almost unstoppable force. There are many lies that come from this unholy union:

> **"God is not good."**
> **"There will never be enough."**
> **"No matter how hard you work, you will never be able to make ends meet."**
> **"You might as well do ___, because in the end it won't matter anyway."**

When fear and deception join together, they result in despair. When you begin to despair, you are heading toward embracing death, and embracing death is agreeing with the Anti-Christ spirit.

Ultimately, the enemy wants to find people who will agree with him. These collaborators then become useful pawns to bring destruction and pain to others. As an artist, you are called to influence and impact the hearts and minds of other people. This is why the enemy works so hard to get the heart of the artist. One only has to search on the internet for a short time to see how bleak and negative most of the art world is. Even more bleak is watching movies and television programs. I hope you are beginning to see how and why the spirit of Anti-Christ wants control over the stories being told. Bombarding the world with negative images and sounds will prevent the world from seeing the good, the true, and the beautiful.

TO RECAP:

- We are in a war, and to be effective warriors we need to understand our enemy.
- Our enemy is the spirit of Anti-Christ.
- The spirit of Anti-Christ denies that Jesus Christ came in the flesh.
- This spirit manifests in antisemitism, in the spirit of the age, and in the death of as many people as possible.
- The chief tools used by the spirit of Anti-Christ are fear and deception.

CHAPTER FOUR

KNOW YOURSELF

After instructing the warrior to "know your enemy" Sun Tzu instructed us to "know yourself." Sadly, most artists have an identity crisis.

Most of my life is spent discussing this with artists. It usually comes out like this:

I know that God has put something inside of me that is great. I know I carry paintings, stories, projects, and ideas that are from God, but I don't know how to make them a reality. I don't know how I can make a living doing these things, and no one seems to think that I can make this my full time job. I don't know how to get from here to there.

After many years of frustration and taking the advice to "get a real job" many artist- warriors lay down their calling and submit to the pressure to be like everybody else. Succumbing to this pressure results in all kinds of suffering, including addiction, sexual brokenness, self-destruction and self-hatred.

I live near the New England coast, and I have been told that when someone catches crabs they need to put a lid on the bucket if you catch only one. One lone crab will escape and run away. But, if you catch two crabs you can leave the bucket uncovered. The second crab will pull the first crab back into the bucket and prevent him from escaping. Often the artist-warrior feels just like those crabs in a bucket. Every time they make that bold choice to move toward their destiny, some outside force will force them back into conformity.

YOUR TRUE IDENTITY

When I was first coming into a level of personal healing, again and again I asked God to reveal to me how he saw me. I had spent several years stuck in an identity crisis and that crisis became a double life. In secret I was involved in all kinds of sexual perversion and drug use. When I asked God to show me who I was, I expected him to show me a broken person who still needed serious "restitution and discipline."

Instead, the Lord spoke to me and said, "I love you, Son of the Most High."

When God looks at us, he looks at how he made us, and what our destiny was created to be. He sees his own image, and the Presence of his Son in us. He sees the beauty of Christ in us, the Hope of Glory.

It might be surprising, but God is not troubled by your failures. Because God is not shocked or disgusted, and because God is also completely aware of them, He is fully able to embrace them. He is able to identify with your brokenness. He entered into broken humanity, and he is able to transform your broken humanity into His image. By coming into contact with your sinful humanity and distorted image, His life giving power brings transformation and healing. Your sin doesn't mar God's glory. Through the cross and blood of Jesus, God's glory destroys your sin. One encounter with Jesus can change you forever.

STRONG MIGHTY WARRIOR

Few people in the Bible had a greater identity crisis than Gideon. The battle he led is one of the greatest "performance art" events in scripture, and it shows how God can do something amazing with a small army and some weird tactics.

Gideon was living in a moment of national crisis for Israel. Because his father's generation had not been faithful to the Lord they had become oppressed by foreign nations. They had ignored the warnings of Moses, forgotten the commitment made under Joshua, and had entered into peace treaties with their enemies. Because they had entered into a dialogue and a relationship with evil, they themselves became evil. The book of Judges says three times that "everyone did what was right in their own eyes." It became so bad that food had to be hidden so that their oppressors, the Midianites, would not take it.

In those days people made wine by digging a cistern in the rock, and pressing the grapes in this vat. Gideon found one of these vats in the ground and began beating out wheat, separating the kernels of wheat from the hulls. This work was normally given to women, and normally was done out in the open.

Today we would say Gideon was "underemployed." I wonder if Gideon was thinking, or even praying in his head about the plans God had for his life. He probably had talents no one knew about. I wonder if Gideon was thinking about the covenant God made with Israel. I wonder if he was asking the question, "How do we get from here to there?"

It says in Judges 6 that the Angel of the Lord came to him and sat and watched him for a while. What Gideon experienced here is called a "theophany," an appearance of the pre-Incarnate Christ, God in the appearance of an angel.

God saw him in this moment of weakness and brokenness, and he watched. Finally, the angel came to Gideon and said, "The Lord is with you Mighty Warrior!"

The Hebrew here is really interesting, because a wooden translation would read something like "The Lord is with you Mighty Valiant Champion" or "Strong Mighty Warrior." The angel was heaping on the superlatives to get the point across.

WHEN GOD CHANGES YOUR NAME

At that moment Gideon did not feel like a warrior or feel mighty. I doubt that he felt valiant. Even so, in that moment God named him. When God names you it is a defining moment. In the naming, Gideon received the blessing of God, and in receiving a new name, the process of change begins.

In this encounter we see a process unfold. Gideon's immediate response is a lot like ours: "If this is true, then why is this bad stuff happening to me?" He follows by asking why the angel came to him, the weakest member of the weakest clan, in the weakest tribe in Israel? Gideon, like us, doesn't believe the new name God has given him.

Even so, the angel says something amazing:

"Tonight Gideon, I hereby commission you to go in this might of yours and deliver Israel."

The Angel of the Lord speaks God's reality to Gideon. Gideon carries something in him that God sees. There is a might that God acknowledges. This person beating wheat in secret carries the seed of the warrior. God's reality is so far from Gideon's reality that it will take some wavering and self-doubt before he embraces it. We see that God is never troubled by Gideon's struggle. This man has a special job to do, and no one else can do it. Because of this, God is patient, and allows him to ask for signs. What we see in this story is the truth that God chooses the weak things of this world to shame the strong. Through weak unlikely people God can receive the greatest glory. God is choosing weak unlikely artists at this moment in history to reveal the greatest glory.

THREE BATTLES

Once Gideon embraces this first layer of his destiny, the angel asks him to destroy the altar to Baal in his town, and to sacrifice his bulls. This request is a challenge to Gideon to embrace the second layer of his destiny. In order to do this, Gideon must work two changes in his life: first, God wants Gideon to deal with his family's generational idolatry, and second, for him to make a clean break with his old life–the life of a farmer.

There are three battles every warrior must face: the battle for the best over the good, the battle over the idols in our lives, and then the battle with the outside world. In this combined act of destroying the altar and sacrificing the bulls, Gideon not only embraces the next step toward his calling, but he also faces all three of these battles.

Baal is a theme we see all over the Old Testament. The people of Israel always seemed to run after Baal. What they were doing was practicing a Canaanite religion that used sexuality to guarantee fertility. Part of Baal worship was the worship of the erect male organ, and anytime you see references to poles used in worship in the Old Testament, you are reading a reference to this Baal/Phallus worship.

When God tells Gideon to go and tear down the altar to Baal and the phallic pole next to it. Gideon is afraid. And he has good reason. Any time that the people of God become comfortable with worshiping God along with idols they can become violent. Deep down people know they are doing wrong and, as in an alcoholic family, truth becomes the enemy. Gideon tears the altar down, but he does it in the middle of the night. There is grace for him, and the townspeople do not punish him. I think deep down they all knew they were doing wrong, and they let Baal fight his own battles. And Gideon is given another name, "Baal Destroyer." But Gideon again suffers self doubt, and God allows him to "put out a fleece" and test his call. Once again, God is not troubled with Gideon's struggle. Whenever God sees Gideon, he sees the Mighty Man of Valor. He knows that inside there is a warrior. It is only a matter of time before the warrior arises. God is never in a hurry, he lets us work out our process on the way to the reality He has placed within us.

RAISING UP AN ARMY

Eventually Gideon does embrace his call, and the Lord instructs him to begin raising an army. What does this army look like? A euphemistic way to describe it is slightly unconventional.

For starters, God tells him to send everyone home who is afraid or who doesn't want to be part of the battle. Two-thirds of his army deserted him. He was left with 10,000. Then the Lord instructed him to do something very strange. He told him to take everyone down to the river and watch them drink. The ones who drink by lifting water to their mouths in their hands are instructed to stay. The ones who get down on their knees to drink are instructed to go home. Gideon is left with 300 men.

Maybe there was more here. Maybe these 300 men were fearless because they were not afraid of what others thought of them. Maybe they were the kind of men who knew who they were, maybe they stood up because they were always prepared. Maybe they were free of the spirit of slavery. Maybe they were the kind of men that were willing to do anything no matter how strange or odd. Maybe they were the kind of people that God could actually use because they had gotten over their "hang-ups."

Regardless, Gideon asks the deserting army to leave their horns and their equipment behind, and he gathers his 300 men.
Many times we overlook little details in scripture. Gideon is left with about 300 ram's horns and about 300 clay jars, and probably about 300 torches. This is not standard equipment for an army.

A DREAM STRATEGY

Gideon overhears a Midianite retelling a dream to his fellow. In the dream a barley cake rolls into the Midianite camp and knocks over all their tents. After the dream is interpreted, Gideon worships God and immediately tells his army. I think you are starting to get the picture that this is not a standard linear battle plan; it is a plan for an army of artistic bent.

What follows is more like a choreographed scene from a 1930s musical than like a battle. Gideon divides his men into three companies. He tells them to take their torches and hide them in the empty pots, and to take the horns left by the men he sent home. He then sends them into the midst of the Midianite camp in the middle of the night, and when they get a cue, he tells them to break their pots, blow their horns, and shout "For the Lord and for Gideon!"

It sounds really crazy, but it worked.

Suddenly in the middle of the night the Midianite army is awakened by the sound of 300 trumpets, the sound of pots breaking and the sudden light of fire all around them in the night. It brought fear and confusion to the camp, and they attacked one another.

Gideon learned who he was, and the nation would have 40 years of peace under his leadership.

CHOOSING TO BELIEVE IN YOUR IDENTITY

Gideon had to make a choice to believe what God was saying about him. For we who are catlled to the frontline, we need to make a decision. Will we embrace the thing that is in us? Will we embrace the call to the creative life, whatever form that may take? This is a dangerous choice to make, it will require sacrifice, change, and may also impact the lives of others.

Lord, in the past I have spent my time like Gideon, not living in the reality of who I am. You have put unusual gifts in me, and there are unusual strategies for the battles we face in this day. I ask you to begin the process of speaking to me, so that I can understand my identity, and my unique place in the battle we face today.

TO RECAP:

- God has put something great inside of you.
- When God looks at you He sees who you were created to be and your destiny.
- One encounter with Jesus will bring transformation.
- When God names you it is a defining moment.

PART TWO

BASIC TRAINING

CHAPTER FIVE

THE WORD MADE FLESH

Living outside of your identity will lead you to confusion and frustration. In the last chapter you saw how Gideon lived in fear because he didn't know that deep inside he was a mighty warrior. For the artist, not understanding your identity could be the source of all kinds of tension and failure in life.

Well, as the proverb says, "a journey of a thousand miles begins with a single step." The first step in this identity journey is understanding the unique role of the artist in God's economy.

Earlier we studied how God revealed himself as the *charash* when he etched the first tablets of law with his finger. God is the designer and constructor of the New Jerusalem. He is the mastermind and executor of the new created order. As we saw in scripture, he spoke and the world came to be. He uttered a word and what did not exist suddenly existed. God the Father is first revealed to us in his very essence as the Creator.

SOMETHING OUT OF NOTHING

Classical theology has a Latin term for this: *ex nihilo sui et subiecti*– *God* makes something out of nothing. This idea of *ex nihilo*, that God speaks and something happens, is one of the central themes of Biblical truth. In the beginning was the WORD. We will see this theme repeated in the scripture again and again as God speaks. Through prophets, angels, teachers, and ultimately, through his own Son, God speaks.

God is always communicating.

And if God is always communicating, we have to also believe that God is a person, and that God is relational. Ultimately this personal communication reveals that God is Love.

COMPLETE COMMUNICATION

The reformers of the sixteenth century understood and reclaimed the centrality of the Word. As we artists know, in their desire to counter the abuses of the Middle Ages, they went too far. God does speak through the written word and the spoken utterance. But God does not limit himself to these means. The limitation placed on communication by the Reformation church created a tension between the artist and the church. It also devalued or ignored some of the most powerful ways the Word comes to us.

Bezalel and Oholiab created a visual revelation of the word. There is no written text inscribed on the Temple or the Tabernacle. The visual presentation, and the worshipers' experience of it was the Word. When we look at the Passover Seder we also encounter the Word in matzo, wine, and bitter herbs. It is the Word with no words. Look at the Jewish prayer shawl, the tallit. Again, no words, and yet it still communicates dwelling under the shadow of the wings of the Father.

When we come into the New Covenant reality, we see an even clearer set of words revealing the Word: the Word comes to us in the Water of Baptism; the Word comes to us in the oil of anointing that not only comes through touch, but fills our sense of smell with the odor of an essential fragrance. And greatest of all, the

Word comes to us in Bread and Wine. That image alone has filled countless pages as saints and thinkers have pondered its multiple meanings.

Of course, there are weaknesses in non-verbal communication, and God would have to send prophets and reformers in every generation to recalibrate the symbols and return them to their original meaning. The verbal and non-verbal need each other. It is often the spoken word that gives life to the experienced Word.

GOD BECOMES THE WORD

So back to God and the artist. Eventually it became time for the greatest performance art piece of all time. God decided to take on flesh. God decided to become the sermon. God became the living example of all that he had said. How did God do it? By very unnatural, yet completely natural means.

The Word was spoken, and a virgin conceived.

But this conception was not *ex nihilo*. This creation was the union between the flesh of a person and the word of God.

That human person becomes our model if we are going to completely embrace our destiny as artists. Mary is our model in the creative life.

CO-LABORING WITH GOD

Every artist has to co-labor with what is within them. And we have to cooperate with the physical realities of our medium. Along with this, we have to accept the limitations of our own skills and choose to accept our creation. A creative idea begins with a germ of an idea, it grows within us, and then it begins to burst forth. Every artist comes to a point where they are not happy until they finish the project they started.

In Gideon's case, we know a lot about his situation at the time of his visitation. Surprisingly, the Gospel writers, Luke and Matthew, do not give us a lot of background information on Mary. In part, this is because they were writing very close to the events that were happening. The land of Israel was under Roman control, with an uneasy peace made with the Hasmonean kings. These kings were not from the family of David, but rather the descendants of Judah Maccabee. It was he who led the revolt against the Greeks, and gave us Hanukkah. He also set up a government that by the time of the New Testament was fairly corrupt. All the people of Israel were crying out for the Messiah to come and rescue them from the outside power of Rome, and the inside corruption of Herod.

Like today, Mary was living in a unique moment.

For the first time in history there was something like global communication and global trade. There was also relative peace and stability. At this pregnant moment, God sends the Angel Gabriel from his presence to a girl in the remote border town Nazareth. And in a similar way to Gideon he gives her an unusual greeting.

"Hail, *kecharitomene!*" (That's "keh-KAY-rit-tow-meen-AY")

That big word needs some unpacking. The "ke-"prefix is important, it indicates that this word is in the Perfect tense. This is something that doesn't exist in English, and indicates that something has been, is now, and will be. "Charis" is the Greek word for grace or gift–the root of our words "charismatic" and "charisma." "-Mene" Indicates that the root of the word is overflowing or abounding. So Mary, like Gideon before, receives a name from an angel–always overflowing with grace. Along with this, he addresses her as a superior. And Luke tells us that Mary was greatly troubled at the angel's greeting. We all face this hurdle, and it is the first important step for the warrior artist. Will you believe and embrace what God says about you? Will you receive the name and the title given to you by God?

Although Mary was troubled, she received the Word.

Gabriel gives her the promise that she will conceive a child, and that child will re-establish the throne of David, and his Kingdom will have no end. Mary's response to this is not disbelief, or even serious struggle. Mary simply asks, "How can this be?"

Gabriel reveals to Mary how God always gives birth to new things, whether they are new souls reborn to eternal life, new moves of God, or new creative acts:

> *The Holy Spirit will come upon you, and the power of the Most high will overshadow you; therefore the child to be born will be called holy, the Son of God. (Luke 1:34)*

BIRTHING THE WORD

Mary encountered the angel Gabriel and Gabriel spoke to her the Word of God. In the speaking, the Holy Spirit began to move in her. When she made the decision, the choice, to embrace the Word and agree with it, her faith activated the Word. At the moment she said, "Let it be to me according to your word" her flesh came into agreement with the Word. At that profound moment the Word was bonded with her DNA and a completely new thing was created. Just like the artist with his or her paints, there was a moment of yielding and then the creative process took over. I imagine Mary, like so many of us creatives, became completely engrossed in her pregnancy. And like the artist, there was a moment of agony where she experienced the pain of childbirth. Only Mary experienced pain when the Word became flesh. Creation caused Mary pain–real physical pain.

An artist experiences agony as the project develops, as the costs mount. Creation requires sacrifice and when it is finished it is embraced by a few but misunderstood and rejected by many. Every creative endeavor is risky. Making the invisible visible is dangerous work. Every act of creativity is an act of Incarnation.

From Bethlehem to Jerusalem Mary learned this. She fled Herod. She saw how the crowds pressed Jesus. She walked with him to the cross. She witnessed the resurrection, and she experienced the first Baptism of the Holy Spirit. Through it all she participated in the new creation. This time it was not *ex nihilo*–out of nothing, but *ex utero*–out of the womb.

MAKING A COMMITMENT

The first five chapters of this book have been an attempt to lay the beginning foundation of understanding where we are and where we are going. Before we move into the next section, we need to confront a simple reality. Do you know who you are, and do you understand the enemy we all face? Have you become a part of the spirit of the age? Have you embraced the name God has given you? As I said in the first chapter, if you hold this book in your hands, you probably are meant to be reading it. I also believe that if you made it this far, you probably have been captivated by something I have written. Do you sense that God might be calling you to this adventure with Him? Are you sensing that stirring that only comes from the Holy Spirit?

If you are, I suggest you put this book down and spend some time waiting on God. Ask the Lord to begin to give you your new name. Ask him to show you who you really are.

> *Abba Father, thank you for the call to join the army of artists in this moment in time. I have not understood all that you have for me, and I have been frustrated at times because I could not walk into my destiny. Too long I have lived under the word "hope deferred makes the heart sick." I ask you to encounter me, to name me, and to shape me. As I embrace your call on my life for this moment, I surrender to your plan. I say, "Let it be to me according to your word." May I be a part of the story you are writing. All this I pray in the name of Jesus Christ, the Living Word.*
> *Amen.*

TO RECAP:

- God first revealed himself as Creator.
- God creates out of nothing through his Word.
- God's Word is verbal and non-verbal.
- Mary is the model of the creative life by saying "yes" to the Word and giving it flesh.
- Every act of creativity is an act of incarnation.

CHAPTER SIX

THE CRUCIFIED ARTIST

Dietrich Bonhoeffer in his spiritual masterpiece *The Cost of Discipleship* made one of the strongest statements found in Christian literature outside the New Testament: "When Christ calls a man he bids him come and die."[5]

You may have started to notice a progression in this book. God is raising up an army of artists, and they have to have a bigger vision than their own creative process or their own sense of creative call. Although these things are necessary for every artist or creative person whether they are believers or not, this is not the end goal for the warrior artist. The warrior artist has to live for the big thing that God is doing, and that will demand sacrifice and at times surrendering his or her personal vision for the vision of the Kingdom.

In other words, you have to take up your cross and follow Jesus.

Many misunderstand the call to bear the cross of Jesus. Maybe the worst misunderstanding is the idea that you are given some difficulty to bear in life. This is really the "stiff upper lip" that we Anglos are taught to exercise. For the artist who is often saddled

---

5 Bonhoeffer, Dietrich, The Cost of Discipleship, New York: Macmillan, 1959. 30

with the idea that their lot in life is to "starve" or be misunderstood, the call to take up the cross can become a twisted notion that really supports the selfishness that is especially strong in creative people.

When Jesus called us to take up our cross, he was inviting us to share in the only path to life—death.

Let me unpack this a little. Embracing the cross means first choosing to die to the ways of this world, and choosing a life of radical obedience to the ways of Jesus. It means choosing his way over our own way, and often choosing the needs of others over the needs of ourselves. One of the fascinating themes I have heard over the years in talking to artists is the repeated direction by God to put down an instrument or surrender a craft. I have met many worship leaders who have had to give away their instruments or who went for a season physically unable to sing. In my own life I spent over 5 years not doing any art at all. God's ways are not our ways. He isn't concerned with your purpose or your mission statement. God is concerned with finding a vehicle who is reliable enough to carry the kingdom.

I know this may seem a little basic, and it may seem out of place in a book for artists, but you have to get this truth into you in order to make a difference. The only people who will be useful in the next season of the church are the people who have come to terms with the hard road to the cross, and embraced the crucified life.

BEING CURRENT WITH HEAVEN

The past 30 years or so the church has ignored this core message of the gospel. Sadly, most of what I see in worship and ministry is simply finding new ways to become relevant to the narcissistic needs of the masses. This is especially strong among worship leaders. There is a constant pressure to be hip and cool and current.

As I have stated earlier, the call to the warrior-artist is to be current with heaven and release heaven into this world. To release the sounds and colors of eternity you will have to be willing to die to earthbound thinking.

St. Paul wrote to the church in Philippi that "many live as enemies of the cross of Christ"(Phil 3:18). Although Paul never identifies these persons, it is clear from the context that he was speaking of a group that was in the church. He was talking about Christians when he says "Their end is destruction, their god is their belly, and they glory in their shame, with minds set on earthly things." (v.19)

When we as artists make the choice to set our minds on the world's ways, especially in the areas of self-promotion and ministry building, we are choosing a very different course than the cross of Christ. Just recently our ministry suffered a major set back because a pastor who was caught up with his vision wanted the location we were using. He stopped at nothing to get it, and in the end succeeded, and several other ministries who were using that space lost access to their work in the city. This pastor believes he will be a success, but it is clear already that he has chosen something foreign to the cross of Christ.

THE 9 YEAR CYCLE

There are ways to build a big ministry, and there are ways to get your name known. You can sell yourself, and you can become a fast rising star. There are dozens of books, videos, and seminars all focused on helping you become a success. A few years ago I heard an interview with John Paul Jackson that described this phenomenon. A ministry that chooses to build apart from the cross of Christ experiences a 9 year life span.

In the first three years a ministry under a visionary leader will begin to grow. If you do it right, you can experience 3 years of continuous growth. Toward the end of that three year period the ministry will begin to become very well known. At about the three year period the second phase of life will begin, this phase will be the plateau. All of the programs established in the first three years will run smoothly. Leadership of much of the original vision will feel competent, and things will hold steady. By the end of the third year of the plateau several things will begin to become clear.

First, many of the people who have been recruited to establish the founder's vision will begin to experience burnout. Some of the core values of that vision will begin to become stale, and for a season there will be new people to replace others who have left the ministry. Then at about the 6 year point, decline will begin to happen in earnest. By the eighth year of this cycle the ministry will begin to rapidly deteriorate into a small group of "true believers." Often the pastor or visionary leader will have already moved on to the next vision and have begun to build something or somewhere else, using the same "tried and true" methods.

Ironically, although many churches and believers have experienced this cycle, few have stopped to recognize it or step back and try an alternative.

John Paul Jackson ended the interview encouraging the viewers to choose to listen to God and follow that guidance, even if it seemed counter intuitive to building a ministry.

This alternative is small, slow, and ugly. After hearing that interview, I personally reassessed my own ministry, and made the choice to adopt a different approach. I made the decision to embrace the cross, and for me personally, that meant learning to listen to God and do what he told me to do. Although it is simple, it has not been easy. Very often it has been painful, and it truly is the way of personal death.

SLOW AND STEADY

When I speak of death I am speaking about choosing a way that may seem inconvenient, or defy accepted norms. Very often the choices I have made have resulted in scorn, ridicule or serious attack from religious leaders. This choice to follow Jesus to the cross has also caused an amazing amount of personal strength and resilience to develop in me, and I have been amazed over the past seven years to see constant, though slow, growth in my work. As the old proverb says, "whatever doesn't kill you makes you stronger."

Along with this, I have found something my friend Kaye Gauder says is correct: "Truth and time go hand in hand." Blessed are you when people speak ill of you and utter all kinds of falsehoods about you. It is a sign that great is your reward in heaven (Matthew 5:11-12). It is also a sign that you are probably on the right path. Why should you not at least experience some of what Jesus experienced--the jealousy, the controversy, and the mistreatment? For many in the creative world these things are an accepted occupational hazard. You might as well go through them for the King and his Kingdom.

Embracing the cross is painful, and you will endure many difficult moments. At the same time you will also experience vindication when someone finally sees they were wrong. You will experience fruit that lasts. One of the tangible ways I measure this fruit is through my email list. Every Friday I send out an email describing what has been happening through my work, Belonging House. In 2006 I began with a list of 6 people. Over the past seven years that list has grown to 270. We have lost people here and there, but the list continues to grow slowly. Over all, the most important number is the actual readership. Most ministry emails average a readership rate of 12%. My emails hover around 40%. Right now I have 100 readers who open and read my emails every week. Yes, it's slow. Yes, it's small. But it is also consistent, and it is consistently growing.

DEALING WITH NARCISSISM

Finally, embracing the cross of Christ gets to the root of our modern society, and a strong tendency among artists–narcissism. David Thomas, in his book *Narcissism: Behind the Mask* [6] describes many of the traits that power hungry narcissists display:

- An obvious self-focus in conversation
- Problems in sustaining satisfying relationships
- Being unaware of their own mental state
- Having difficulty empathizing with others
- Having difficulties separating themselves from others
- Hypersensitivity to any insults or imagined insults
- A tendency toward shame rather than guilt
- Haughty body language
- Flattery towards people who admire and affirm them
- Detesting those who do not admire them
- Using other people without considering the cost of doing so
- Pretending to be more important than they really are
- Subtle and persistent bragging and exaggerating their achievements
- Claiming to be an "expert" at many things
- Inability to view the world from the perspective of other people
- Inability to show remorse or gratitude

---

6 Thomas, David, *Narcissism: Behind the Mask*. Sussex, UK: Book Guild, 2010. 33

There is only one real cure for narcissism; true repentance. Along with this, there is only one recovery system for the narcissistic tendency in all of us. Our only hope if we are going to be useful for the kingdom is to take up our cross, die with Jesus to our own desires, and follow him.

THE PATH TO LIFE

Of course, all of this cross business can make a person excessively serious. Embracing the cross is not an excuse for a morbid fascination with death or bloody religious pictures. Embracing the cross and choosing death really is the path to life.

"Truly, truly I say to you, unless a grain of wheat falls to the earth and dies, it remains alone; but if it dies it bears much fruit" (John 12:24).

In this verse we are offered not only the promise of multiplication, we are offered the promise of a cure for aching loneliness. We are offered as Paul described "the fellowship of his sufferings." Jesus promises us that he will be with us. And as we shall see in the next chapter, the crucified life makes way for the promise of Jesus in us.

TO RECAP:

- The warrior artist is called to the only path that leads to life–the cross.
- The only people who will be useful in the next season of the church are the people who have come to terms with the hard road to the cross, and embraced the crucified life.
- To release the sounds and colors of eternity you will have to be willing to die to earthbound thinking.
- Embracing the cross of Christ addresses the root of our modern society, and a strong narcissistic tendency among artists.
- The only one real cure for narcissism is true repentance.

CHAPTER SEVEN

LIVING FROM THE INSIDE OUT

In the last chapter I described the call to come and die. As I mentioned, the only way to experience life is to embrace death. Let me rephrase this,

It is only in letting go that you can receive.

I know this sounds very cryptic. It is really very simple.

The precious part of you is on the inside. From before time and eternity, God has always seen that part of you. There is a real you and a false you. Sadly many of us cultivate the false self so that we can survive or get ahead in life. When you choose to embrace the cross of Christ and die, you are dying to your false self. In dying you give that inner part of you the ability to rise to the surface, and in rising, the resurrection power of God begins to flow. I have seen in my own life how my own basic abilities and talents become supernatural tools for God to use after I surrendered them. Usually I am the one who is most surprised by what God did through my life.

The warrior artist has to embrace this most important truth in the gospel message:

God works from the inside out.

Man works from the outside in. Paul describes God's way of working in Colossians 1:27 when he described "Christ in you the hope of glory." This is the promise of the New Covenant, and it is going to be the central reality of the next season in the church. Jesus lives inside of you, and he wants to inhabit your work–the work of the arts.

JESUS IN YOU

A few years ago I began a bullet list of things that result if Jesus really lives in me. They became a series of blog posts that received a lot of feedback.

If Jesus really lives in you, then:
- The Word of God Incarnate flows inside you. The Prince of Peace is in you to bring peace.
- The fountain of Living Water flows in you.
- The Bread of Life is feeding you.
- The Resurrection and the Life is in you to give you life, healing, and wholeness.
- You are blessed because the Father said "This is my beloved Son, in whom I am well pleased."
- You have all authority to do what God has given you to do, because the King of Kings lives in you.
- You are able to cast out the devil because the name of Jesus is above every other name.
- You can be free from sin because Jesus is free from sin, and he lives in you.
- You can love others, because God is love, and God lives in you.
- You do not have to be beaten about by life, because greater is He that is IN you than he that is in the world.

Everything Jesus did by becoming a man, by living a sinless life, by suffering and dying, and by rising again is available to you right now. Paul said that the same Spirit that raised Jesus from the dead is in you, giving life to your mortal bodies. This list became an extended project as I began looking at key passages in the New Testament. I started looking for practical promises about the promise of Christ in me.

Here is the list I made based on the eighth chapter of Paul's letter to the Romans:
- You are not condemned (Romans 8:1).
- You are free from sin and death (Romans 8:2).
- Your spirit is alive because of His righteousness (Romans 8:10).
- The same power that raised Jesus from the dead is in you (Romans 8:11).
- And He who raised Jesus from the dead will give life to your body (Romans 8:11).
- You are God's son (Romans 8:14).
- You are free from the spirit of slavery (Romans 8:15).
- You do not have to live in fear (Romans 8:15)
- You will receive an inheritance from God (Romans 8:17).
- You will be glorified (Romans 8:18).
- You will experience glorious liberty (Romans 8:21).
- Your body will be redeemed (Romans 8:23).
- The Holy Spirit will give you help when you are weak (Romans 8:26).
- The Holy Spirit prays to God on your behalf (Romans 8:27).
- Everything will work out for good in your life (Romans 8:28).
- You will begin to take on the shape of the image of Jesus (Romans 8:29).
- God has called you (Romans 8:30).
- God has justified you (Roman 8:30).

I made another list from John chapter 14:

- You will do the works that Jesus did (John 14:12)
- You will do greater works than Jesus did (John 14:12)
- What ever you ask God for in Jesus' name he will do (John 14:13)
- The Spirit of Truth lives in you (John14:17)
- You are not abandoned (John 14:18)
- You live because Jesus lives in you (John 14:19)
- Jesus will love you, and manifest himself to you (John 14:21)
- Jesus (and the Father) makes his home in you (John 14:23)
- You will hear the Father's voice (John 14:23)
- The Holy Spirit will teach you all things (John 14:26)
- The Holy Spirit will remind you of all that Jesus said (John 14:26)
- Jesus will give you his peace (John 14:27)

After this third list, I took a break from the project. Honestly, I knew more than I was experiencing. Our challenge is to move from "knowing" in the Greco-Roman Western sense–the intellectual knowledge of facts–to "knowing" in the Hebrew sense–the intimate experience of a truth. The word "yada" that is translated "know" in the Bible actually refers to the knowing a man and a woman experience when they conceive a child. Once again, this is an inside out reality. It is a deep intimate knowledge.

BEING ANOINTED

When we are saturated in the reality of God in us, then everything we do becomes ministry. We begin to function in our anointing. It is like a river running out of us. The anointing of God flows out of the inner life of Jesus flowing in us. When this happens a painting can be used by God to heal people. A song, even a simple one, can be used to release people from bondage. A simple act can suddenly become a powerful tool of ministry. Your life as an artist suddenly becomes a supernatural activity.

Few people have spoken and written more about the anointing than R.T. Kendall.[7] On the evening of November 11, 2011 I was painting at the Old South Church in Newburyport, Massachusetts. I felt a gentle hand on my shoulder. I looked to see who was standing there and heard the voice of R.T. Kendall in my ear.

"That," R.T. whispered while pointing to my painting, "is your anointing."

It doesn't take long for an average person to see the pain, confusion, and brokenness pouring out of many artists. The inner state of the artist lines the walls of galleries all over the world. In the same way, it also doesn't take long for a person to see that much of what passes for "Christian Art" is flowing out of an equally troubled soul. At best, much of this art is shallow. These paintings of rainbows, lighthouses, lions and doves are an expression of men and women who have never experienced the depths of the spiritual life. They are as disconnected from God as the "secular" artist.

In order to express a connection with God, and be a bearer of heaven, you have to go through the three step process of saying "yes" to God. First, you have to say yes like Mary did. You have to say yes to being a willing vessel, to be willing to let God become flesh through you. After this, you need to say "yes" like Jesus did in the Garden of Gethsemane. You have to say yes to the cross, you have to go low, and look right at your own death and embrace it.

---

7 There is not space in this book to do justice to the topic of the anointing of the Holy Spirit. I recommend *The Anointing* by R.T. Kendall, Nashville, TN: Thomas Nelson, 1999.

Finally, you need to say "yes" the way the apostles said yes in the upper room. You need to be empowered and filled with the Holy Spirit. Jesus living in you is not a magical concept, or even a theological truth. Jesus living in you is a practical, experiential **requirement** for you to live out the ministry you have been called to. Your ministry is *you being you,* as an artist, empowered by the Holy Spirit.

A BURNING HEART

John Wesley once said, "Get on fire for God and all the world will come and watch you burn."

There is only one way to burn, and that is by being filled with the Holy Spirit. I guess it is no surprise that the moment Wesley's faith came to life he said his "heart was strangely warmed."

Before you can become a warrior artist, you need to have an experience with the Holy Spirit. This only happens by faith, but often there is a physical witness that comes with the faith. If you have been filled with the Holy Spirit, you need to keep on being filled. As Paul told Timothy, you need to "stir up the gift of God that is within you" (II Timothy 1:6).

One of the ways you can do this is through a simple prayer that has become one of my favorites.

> *Jesus, I believe that You are in me, and I am in You.*
> *If I am in You, then I am in my Father, and my*
> *Father is in Me, just as You are in the Father. Thank*
> *you that I abide in You, and Your word abides in me.*
> *Because of this I can ask anything in Your Name, I*

can do greater things than You did, I can love others
as You have loved me, and by this Your Father is
glorified. Come Holy Spirit, and fill me. I receive you
now by faith to live in me, empower me, and move
through me.
Amen.

After this, you need to take a few moments to wait on God. I also suggest you take the time to speak out the statements in the lists earlier in this chapter, making them personal to yourself.

TO RECAP:

- God works from the inside out.
- The power to do ministry is from Jesus living inside of you.
- The anointing of God causes your natural life to become ministry.
- Being filled with the Holy Spirit is a requirement to do the ministry you are called to.

CHAPTER EIGHT

SITTING IN HEAVEN

In the previous chapters we have been exploring how closely the artist must identify with Christ. God is calling you to be a "little Christ," a living breathing example of who he is.

You have probably begun to recognize the pattern that is developing in this book. The warrior artist is called to embrace the Incarnation, surrender to Crucifixion, and live in Resurrection. It is probably obvious then, that we must talk about living with Christ in heavenly places. God is calling us to also share in the Ascension.

> But God, who is rich in mercy, out of the great love with which he loved us, even when we were dead through our trespasses, made us alive together with Christ (by grace you have been saved), and raised us up with him, and made us sit with him in the heavenly places in Christ Jesus, that in the coming ages he might show the immeasurable riches of his grace in kindness toward us in Christ Jesus. (Ephesians 2:4-7)

If Jesus really lives in you, and if Jesus has descended to the lowest depths of humanity, it would only make sense that Jesus raised us up with him when he ascended into heaven.

The warrior artist is called to bring the reality of heaven into this fallen world.

Everything that heaven touches is changed. In order for this to happen, we have to begin to cultivate the experience of heaven in our own lives.

Some of the old saints in the Holiness Movement of the late nineteenth and early twentieth centuries sometimes spoke of living an "ascended lifestyle." I was fortunate as a very young man to meet and know a number of elderly people who had been touched by this move of God. The memory of their real holiness of life is still burned into my soul. These men and women were full of love. They experienced answered prayer. They were pure, clean, and full of sanctity. They were also free of the legalism that masquerades as holiness.

The witness of these holy men and women has become even more pronounced to me as the church around me continues to descend into moral and spiritual decay.

A HIGHER REALITY

There is a spiritual reality to being seated with Christ in heavenly places. This is not a fine point of theology. It is a calling that we are summoned to experience.
So how do we experience it?

Paul prayed in the first chapter of Ephesians for his readers to receive a spirit of wisdom and revelation. In truth, in order for us to experience the reality of heaven, we need the windows of revelation to open to us. The New Testament reveals a lot about the Kingdom of Heaven. We need to start reading with the eyes of our heart being enlightened.

The window of revelation begins when we first make the decision to change our perspective. The earth-bound perspective tells us we need to "try harder" to rise above our human situation. This effort to rise above our circumstances is the root of man centered religion. I can't tell you how many times I have been in meetings where people believed if they simply prayed the right way or prayed hard enough they would "get the breakthrough" and revival would come.

You cannot bring the breakthrough, and you can't make it happen. To get a revelation of heaven you have to go back to the lesson about the cross. You have to let go of any belief that it depends on you to make it happen, and you have to accept the reality that God has to release it to you. If you are a creative person, or tend to being a perfectionist, this will be especially difficult. In order to get revelation, you need to let go of control.

OPEN HEAVEN

In 2004 I experienced a major life crisis and my spiritual advisor gave me this advice: "Listen to the Lord, and do what He tells you." I was so desperate that I actually took his advice. There were many adventures along the way as I slowly listened to God. To my surprise, I began to experience "open heaven" moments.

The most dramatic one happened in 2006. One of the things the Lord instructed me to do was dance during my daily worship time. I was very reluctant, but one day I did begin to dance. This experience I recounted in detail in my first book *The Glory of a Wasted Life.*

> At first, I thought it was just my imagination, but soon I was overwhelmed by the weightiness of the atmosphere. What I saw was a place where the sky was not blue, but a

luminous gold. There were mountains all around, and they too seemed to be made of a form of gold. In the center of this valley were four golden lamp stands, and around the lamps were clouds of incense. Above the lamp stands was what looked like a disc made of pure light. This light was a deep emerald green, and the edge of the disc was like the light coming from a prism forming the spectrum. As the Bible describes, there was a sea of emerald, encircled by a rainbow. The disc floated in air, and on the disc was a throne, and there was a person on the throne, but I could not see him. I don't think I could look at him. I kept looking down.

Around the pillars were four creatures, the size of elephants. They were an intense ultramarine blue. They had wings that were like eagle's wings, but they were deep red, purple, blue, and gold. The creatures were highly animated, and seemed to be playful, even though they were the size of monsters. Strangely, they seemed to have eyes on every side. The thing that has perplexed me the most about the vision is the depth and intensity of the colors. There is no way to capture the brilliance of what I saw. I have tried with my paints and my pencils to capture it, only to give up in frustration.

I must have been standing on a high cliff above the scene because I saw a massive crowd of millions upon millions of people. From my vantage point, they were all wearing white robes. They were dancing in concentric circles around the throne, and their hands were all joined. It looked as if they all doing the same dance, in beautiful choreography. They were filled with a rapturous joy.

As I began to take all of this in, I was lifted off my feet and brought down to the farthest circle. As I approached the crowd, I saw that the people were not wearing white robes, but their own clothes. They were not doing the same dance, but each was doing their own dance. This really puzzled me, since they continued to hold hands. In the crowd, I saw faces of friends who had recently died, and even recognizable saints. They were all completely whole and alive.

At that moment, I looked up and noticed a figure approaching me. He was flying, and I assumed that he was an angel. As he got nearer, he began to communicate with me, but it was not in speech as we communicate in this world. It was almost as if it were by "telepathy." He told me to look down at the ground. Around me were bricks made of gold. The ground was paved with gold bricks.

"Do you see the ground? Do not worry about your finances. All of your financial problems, your debt, your house and everything else are worth less than one brick — even a stone from this place."

I began to be aware of my lack of faith and the fear that had dictated most of my life. I began to weep.

As the angel got closer, I discovered that he was made out of what seemed to be pure fire. His face, eyes, wings, and hands were all pure fire; he was white, but it was a white fire. He was a living flame. As he approached, I began to take in the size of this being. He must have been about twelve feet tall. I began to bow down, and he told me to stand up. In this encounter I learned a lot about angels. I learned they come to do a job, and they do it with pure force! I also learned they come with messages, and at times I couldn't tell if he was speaking on behalf of himself or the Lord.

"Stand up and do not weep," he said. "You do not know who you are."
Then he reached out, touched my eyes and my ears, and I could see and hear more clearly. He put a white robe on me and touched my heart. My heart burned within me, and it seemed as if my chest cavity was enlarged so I could receive more of the love being poured in. I was given colorful wings.

The rest of the vision began to grow dim as he got closer. And he began to speak with me. *I am calling you to raise up an army of artists to build Jesus a throne in the earth.*[8]

That experience began to change my perspective on living in the heavenly reality. My understanding of what was possible suddenly shifted from what I was able to do in my own strength to what God was able to do through me. There is more available to us than we can comprehend. The challenge is getting that heavenly reality into this earthly one.

LIVING THERE HERE

As I mentioned earlier, there is a moral dimension to all this. If we really grasp who we are, and where we are seated, it is going to change the way we live our lives. Take a minute and consider some realities about heaven.

---

8 Otto, Christ John, *The Glory of a Wasted Life*. BookSurge, 2008. 42

In heaven there is no death or decay. In heaven there is no gossip. In heaven no one speaks critically of others. In heaven every one is walking into the fullness of who they were created to be. In heaven there are no hidden things–everything is full of light, and the light of revelation is experienced by every one. There are no locks in heaven, because there is no theft. There is no divorce. There are no tears. There is no pain, disease, or brokenness. There is no dust in heaven, because dust is a byproduct of death.

Like the dance I described, there are millions of people each doing the thing they were created to do. As each one fulfills their role, there is perfect interconnected unity. That unity happens around the throne, because in heaven everything and everyone is full of the One at the center of the Throne. He fills all, and is in all.

As I said earlier, if Jesus really lives in you, then you are sitting with him. You are where he is, in heaven. You are called to share in what he is doing, interceding to the Father on behalf of creation. You are called to share in the intimate love the Father has for the Son. You are called to be a vessel of the sights, sounds, smells, and vibrations of the heavenly realm. Jesus, seated in heaven, wants to reign in and through you, his vessel.

Of course, our challenge is always that we experience less than we know. God's call on the artist is to be the vehicle that brings heaven into places where heaven hasn't been reigning. How do we get from there to here after we have the revelation?

There is a practical answer, and I will unpack this in the next chapter. But before that let's pray for that experience of revelation.

*I do not cease to give thanks for you, remembering
you in my prayers, that the God of our Lord Jesus
Christ, the Father of glory, may give you a spirit of
wisdom and of revelation in the knowledge of him,
having the eyes of your hearts enlightened, that you
may know what is the hope to which he has called
you, what are the riches of his glorious inheritance in
the saints, and what is the immeasurable greatness
of his power in us who believe, according to the
working of his great might which he accomplished in
Christ when he raised him from the dead and made
him sit at his right hand in the heavenly places,
far above all rule and authority and power and
dominion, and above every name that is named, not
only in this age but also in that which is to come;
and he has put all things under his feet and has
made him the head over all things for the church,
which is his body, the fulness of him who fills all in
all. Amen!*
(Ephesians 1:16-23).

TO RECAP:
- We are called to experience the Ascension.
- The warrior artist is called to bring the reality of heaven to earth.
- An understanding of heaven will impact the way we live our lives here.

CHAPTER NINE

HOLY PEOPLE, HOLY THINGS

Grace is the currency of heaven. In classical language, the experience of this currency comes to us through things called "the means of grace." In this chapter I want to unpack these two sentences, and hopefully begin to bring us full circle back to the role of the artisan in scripture and what that means for today.

GRACE IS THE CURRENCY OF HEAVEN.

Since the Protestant Reformation grace has often been defined as "God's unmerited favor." Many of the Protestant reformers were lawyers, and they often described grace in legal terms. The image of the law court and being found "not guilty" is the extent many Christians know of grace. And it is true, having the experience of forgiveness and justification is definitely grace. It is the unmerited favor of God to us who really do not deserve it.

Even though grace can be a state that we enter into, grace can also be a substance that we experience. This dynamic understanding of grace is what I am describing when I talk about the currency of heaven. It is this grace that we experience when we talk about the "movement" of the Holy Spirit. The currency of heaven is God's Person, Presence, and Power. This is the grace that Jesus described flowing out of him when the woman touched the fringe of his garment and was healed. In this sense, grace is an experiential "substance."

In the Middle Ages the dynamic concept of grace was abused so much that the first wave of reformers over-reacted. Grace became a static concept that was limited to the experience of coming to Christ. After that, in the popular mind, you were on your own to live out the Christian life.

GET IN THE FLOW

This began to change with John Wesley, who began talking about grace in a dynamic way. The renewal movements that have continued to flow out of the Methodist revivals–the Holiness, Pentecostal, and Charismatic movements, all share a common understanding that grace is dynamic. It flows.

I am describing the experiential Presence, Power, and Person of the Holy Spirit. He is the currency of heaven, and He brings the realities of the heavenly realm into our realm. It is through the Holy Spirit that we can be living in Jesus, and also sitting in heaven. And it is through the grace of the Holy Spirit, the unmerited favor of His Presence, that we can bring heaven to earth.

Charismatic Christians understand this because they have often experienced grace in tangible ways through physical things.

The "Means of Grace" is a classical term that essentially means God uses actions and things to communicate his Person, Presence, and Power. Please don't miss this point, because it is essential for every warrior artist to understand.

God uses actions and things to communicate his Person, Presence, and Power.

Another way of talking about this is to talk about the "Sacramental Principle." The Book of Common Prayer describes a sacrament as "an outward and visible sign of an inward and spiritual grace." Until the Reformation, this was the central way that many Christians experienced God.

Eventually, there came to be a standard list of seven sacraments that were believed to be the normal ways that people experienced grace:

- Baptism (Matthew 28:19)
- Holy Communion (Luke 22:19-20)
- Confirmation, or the laying on of hands to be filled with the Holy Spirit (Acts 8:17)
- Confession of Sin and Forgiveness (James 5:16)
- Christian Marriage (John 2:1)
- Anointing and Laying hands on the Sick for healing (James 5:14)
- Laying on of Hands in Ordination to ministry. (2 Timothy 2:6)

All of these are described at various places in the New Testament.

THE MEANS OF GRACE

John Wesley created another list of what he called the "Means of Grace." He felt that all Christians would experience and continue walking in a dynamic relationship with God if they did these things: pray; read the Bible; regularly receive Holy Communion; and meet regularly with other Christians to confess their sins, hold each other accountable, and pray for one another.

What becomes clear is that God uses two things to communicate grace. God uses objects when the Holy Spirit is invited to use them--water, bread, wine, and oil. He also uses people who are filled with the Holy Spirit. Notice how many times touching another person is part of that first list. The other aspect of all of these is the centrality of relationships. The currency of heaven is released when we have clear relationships with God and with other believers.

> **God uses holy people and holy things to communicate his Person, Presence and Power.**

It is very simple.

Over time another list emerged, and this list became what is known as "sacramentals." These are things that are not really commanded in scripture, but people have found that God uses them powerfully too. One of the big ones is Holy Water–water that has been mixed with blessed salt and then is blessed for healing. I have personally witnessed the consistent power that God extends through Holy Water. Other things that fall into this category are flags, banners, the blowing of the Shofar, and symbolic actions. This isn't magic, it is God responding to our faith as we agree with him. The danger, and also the abuse, occurs when we raise these extra things above the core means of grace. In other words, we can't focus on flags and banners if we aren't sharing Holy Communion regularly.

My ministry is based in Salem, Massachusetts. Over the years, groups from around the country have come to pray here and in Greater Boston. Often when I describe my work, these visitors are a little disappointed because I focus on confessing sin from the past and leading small groups in Holy Communion at key locations. I don't do a lot of dramatic praying, and rarely do I use "props" like flags, staffs, and shofars (although I can point to moments when we have used all of these things). It is the simple things–focusing on the cross of Jesus, healing relationships, and forgiving sin–that are the most powerful in releasing the currency of heaven.

So what does this have to do with artists?

God is raising up an army. The army arising has to be able to receive and deliver the currency of heaven.

In other words, YOU are a means of grace.

My guess is, if you are an artist, you either make things or make music. Remember the "charash" artisans I described in chapter 2? God is calling men and women to rise up and be the means of grace in this hour. Your craft, your calling and your very person are called to be the vehicle of the Person, Presence and Power of God. In order for that to happen you have to be centered and flowing in the grace of God. There are some very practical steps you need to take if you are going to be the means of grace.

First, if you have made decision to follow Jesus but you have not been baptized, you need to make this step. The Bible instructs us to repent and be baptized, and all the other grace flows from this first one.

Second, you cannot be a warrior if your spirit is "flabby." You need a regular spiritual workout–daily prayer and Bible study. I believe that artists, especially those who consider themselves "prophetic artists" need to be in the Bible. You need to see the images and metaphors of scripture refreshing your mind and imagination. You need to be in a constant conversation with God, hearing his voice, and responding with obedience. I personally follow the lectionary, an ordered daily reading of the Bible that causes me to go through most of the Bible in year.

If you want a deeper revelation of God and heaven, the Bible is your guide. If you want to learn how to hear God clearly, you have to begin with the Bible. The Bible is like a tuner that helps you hear the frequency of heaven. The Bible helps establish the path in your soul that the Holy Spirit can use to clarify your hearing. The Bible will also help you keep from getting distracted by lesser things. [9]

Third, you need to be in community with others. If you aren't part of a healthy church, drop this book and go find one. You need to be in relationships with others. This is especially difficult for creative people because relationships are painful, and sometimes artists are misunderstood. It is also easy for artists to be alone and solitary. I believe it is important to be in a small group. Personally, having a regular person who serves as my "confessor" has been very helpful. I have also been blessed to have a small group of intercessors who pray for me regularly.

Finally, I have come to believe strongly that Holy Communion is essential. I am so thankful that God is restoring an appreciation and understanding of Holy Communion to many in the Protestant church. The regular reception of the Body and Blood of Jesus has been one of the most transformative experiences in my life. I am confident it will have a similar effect on your life.

All of these things begin to create a conduit in your life that allows heaven to flow. When grace begins to flow into your life, it freely begins to flow out to others through all that you do. Your call is to be a means of grace for this broken and hurting world. You are called to be a house of prayer. You are called to be the Tabernacle of David. You are called to bear the Presence, Power, and Person of God wherever you go.

---

9 There are many online resources to make reading through the Bible simple. I highly recommend *Bookofcommonprayer.net* and *divineoffice.org*.

Soul of Christ, sanctify me.
Body of Christ, save me.
Blood of Christ, inebriate me.
Water from Christ's side, wash me.
Passion of Christ, strengthen me.
O good Jesus, hear me.
Within your wounds hide me.
Suffer me not to be separated from you.
From the malicious enemy defend me.
In the hour of my death call me,
and bid me come unto you;
That I may praise you with your saints
and with your angels forever and ever,
Amen.

TO RECAP:

- Grace is the currency of heaven.
- Grace is a substance we can experience: the Person, Power and Presence of God.
- The Holy Spirit uses actions and things to transmit grace.
- God uses holy people and holy things to transmit grace.

PART THREE

THE WEAPONS OF
OUR WARFARE

*For though we live in the world, we are not carrying
on a worldly war for the weapons of our warfare
are not worldly, but have divine power to destroy
strongholds. We destroy arguments and every proud
obstacle to the knowledge of God, and take every
thought captive to obey Christ.*

II Corinthians 10:3-5

CHAPTER TEN

EXCELLENCE

In this third section of *An Army Arising* I am going to address some of the key practical things we need to do to succeed in the very strange war we are fighting. Some of these instructions are obvious, and others are counter-intuitive. One of the most obvious tools in our arsenal is the weapon of Excellence.

Excellence is ultimately doing what you love and doing it well.

Judy Garland once said, "Always be a first-rate version of yourself, instead of a second rate version of somebody else." This is the heart of excellence.

You can't truly live an excellent life until you embrace the truth that God knows you and has put something in you that is unique. As you lay aside fear and walk toward your destiny, you will begin to see that God really wants you to do the thing you love, be the person you were made to be and walk in the reality of your "YOUness."

What I am talking about is the real you, your true self. The true self is the person you are deep inside. It is the unique expression of the image of God in you, that can only be released through that amazing combination of DNA, talent, and experience that makes you unique.

BEING YOURSELF

One of the writers who has impacted me greatly is Thomas Merton. In his masterpiece *New Seeds of Contemplation,* Merton describes what it means to walk into the real you.

> A TREE gives glory to God by being a tree. For in being what God means it to be it is obeying Him. It "consents," so to speak, to His creative love. It is expressing an idea which is in God and which is not distinct from the essence of God, and therefore a tree imitates God by being a tree.
>
> The more a tree is like itself, the more it is like Him. If it tried to be like something else which it was never intended to be, it would be less like God and therefore it would give Him less glory. . .
>
> . . . For me to be a saint means to be myself. Therefore the problem of sanctity and salvation is in fact the problem of finding out who I am and of discovering my true self. Trees and animals have no problem. God makes them what they are without consulting them, and they are perfectly satisfied. With us it is different. God leaves us free to be whatever we like. We can be ourselves or not, as we please. We are at liberty to be real, or to be unreal. We may be true or false, the choice is ours.[10]

The challenge that many of us face is the pressure to conform, and that conformity can not only kill us, but also kill any chance of our becoming excellent.

---

10 Merton, Thomas, *New Seeds of Contemplation,* pp. 31, 33-34, Norton: Kindle Edition.

SELLING OUT

In 1997 this point became very clear to me when I was beginning the ordination process in the Episcopal church. The political forces that would result in a world wide split in the denomination were already in motion. After a few meetings with officials in the ordination process, it was becoming clear I was going to have to compromise my personal faith and also decisions I had made regarding sexuality. My sponsoring priest pulled me aside and said "Just tell the committee whatever they want to hear, and do whatever they tell you to do. You need to get through the ordination process, and once you are ordained you can do whatever you want."

My response was, "You want me to become a priest. God wants me to become a saint."

I couldn't "sell out" to get ordained. I knew that after ordination my message would always be compromised, and I also knew that if I did some of what they were asking me, I could lose my relationship with God.

"Selling out" and compromise are two ways to describe the same thing: assimilation. Assimilation is the process of becoming like the environment around you. Fear is often what fuels assimilation.

One of the key passages of scripture for my life and ministry is from Romans chapter 8.

> For all who are led by the Spirit of God are sons of God.
> For you did not receive the spirit of slavery to fall back into
> fear, but you have received the spirit of sonship. When we
> cry 'Abba, Father!' it is the Spirit himself bearing witness

with our spirit that we are children of God, and if children, then heirs, heirs of God and fellow heirs with Christ, provided we suffer with him in order that we may also be glorified with him.
(Romans 8:14-17)

The choice before us to sell out and compromise is birthed out of a general insecurity that God is good, and that we are his children. But if we can get a hold of this truth that we are His sons and that He is a good father, we can have confidence that God is not only with us, God is in us. Then we can explore our true selves and pursue his call to us without fear.

However, choosing to be your true self and being true to yourself will come with a price. For the creative person there is often the real call to be alone, not follow the crowd, or not do what is popular. If you decide to do this, you are taking the step toward finding and doing what you love.

After you embrace the idea of becoming your true self, there is a process of actually doing it. And looking for the thing you are called to do is part of that process.

YOUR TRUE SELF RELEASES THE ANOINTING

I mentioned earlier the moment when R.T. Kendall pointed out that my anointing was clear when I was painting. He was actually confirming what I already knew, but had neglected. At the time he said this, I was working for a crisis pregnancy center in Boston. I had also devoted several years to leading prayer in and around the city. But I was not focused on art.

R.T. Kendall was using a term found throughout scripture, the anointing, to describe what happens when I do the thing I am called to do. Because I am embracing my primary call, the Holy Spirit is present in a unique way, and this presence impacts others. Because of this, I have watched over the years how my paintings have touched others. I have seen people experience emotional and physical healing through the paintings, and I have seen how some of the paintings take on their own lives. This is the anointing, and it is also a core part of my true self.

Last year I received an extraordinary package in the mail. It was a large mailing tube. When I opened it I found many rolled up pieces of paper. They were drawings that I did while I was in kindergarten. My teacher had saved them for nearly 40 years and felt that I needed to have them. She also described how I told stories while I painted as a child, and the entire class would sit quietly and watch. When she found out what I do now, she was not surprised. "You have been painting in front of large groups your entire life."

The second part of living a life of excellence is doing what you do well.

If you are reading this book, you probably have a natural talent in some area. But, every talent needs to be developed. The second, and sometimes more critical, part of excellence is having the diligence to develop your gift. This requires practice and a lot of little choices.

In the front cover of my prayer book, I wrote a quotation from Aristotle that sums this up: "We are what we repeatedly do. Excellence therefore, is not an act, but a habit."

In seminary I was blessed to study preaching with Dr. Ellsworth Kalas. His class was unique—we were not allowed to preach with notes ("Why do you expect others to remember your sermon if you can't remember it," he would say). We were also expected to preach one point sermons. Finally, we were required to preach from the same text as every other member of the class.

One day one of the students in the class began to preach and was very sloppy with his language. He was using slang, using note cards, and was overall very poorly dressed. As we discussed the student's sermon in the class, the preacher defended himself by saying, "Those are all just little things."

Dr. Kalas looked at the student in his fatherly way and said, "Yes, but life is made up of lots of little things."

KAIZEN

A life of little choices and daily improvements will eventually bring you to a place of superior performance. The Japanese call this idea "Kaizen."

Essentially, every day you choose one small manageable area to improve, and you improve that small thing. The next day you choose another small thing to improve. And every day you make the choice to improve one more small area. Eventually, you will discover you have made major improvements.

Practicing Kaizen will also break the back of perfectionism—a deadly habit for artists. Perfectionism is setting unreachable goals for yourself and then attempting to reach them through control and effort. Eventually you will fail if you do this, and it will begin a destructive cycle of failure and self hatred. And because you are creative, you will always see the part that is not perfect or complete, and then become even more fixated on your failure. Talk about a death spiral.

Another side-effect of perfectionism is the way it freezes people. Because the goal of absolute perfection is impossible, many creatives are unable to start a project for fear of failure. Anything worth doing is worth doing in such a way that you accept your limitations. If you step out and try something, even if it is a poor attempt, you will learn something in the process. The next project will be improved from the last experiment. KAIZEN!

INSIDE OUT EXCELLENCE

My dear friend, Alice Stewart taught me one of the most amazing lessons about little choices and about real excellence. We were looking at a show of final projects created by fashion design students. Alice shook her head in disapproval at several of the costumes.

"Those are poorly constructed. A good seamstress makes the inside seams look as good as the exterior."

Excellence is really tested when no one is looking. That hidden choice to do a job well, or make the consistent choice will be obvious under pressure. It is the little habits of excellence that make the difference in the moment it matters. These little choices include:

- choosing to practice
- choosing to continually learn new skills or improve old ones
- choosing to eliminate activities and habits that are not aligned with your true self.
- choosing to do your best no matter what the outcome
- choosing not to compromise

Little choices added to your natural talent and energized by God's anointing will result in a life of excellence!

As I said at the beginning of this chapter, excellence is doing what you love and doing it well. Excellence will cause others to come and see what you are doing. It may take time, but excellence is what will set you apart.

AN UNLIKELY STAR

In the late 1940's a tall, big boned woman began looking for a something to occupy her time while her husband was working for the diplomatic corps in France. On a whim, she decided to take cooking classes. Finding the classes offered to society matrons dull, she enrolled in classes for professional chefs offered to American G.I.'s in the basement of Le Cordon Bleu in Paris. Although she didn't have a natural talent, she was committed, and she worked hard. She found the thing she loved to do, and set out to do it well.

Eventually she was given the opportunity to adapt a French cookbook for the U.S. market. Her adaptation eventually became a complete re-write, and her book became famous. You know I am speaking of Julia Child. In the early 1960s she was given an opportunity to record an educational television show in Boston. That show, *The French Chef* is still on the air in reruns, and here in Boston we can watch Julia's first episodes in black and white each Saturday. Her kitchen is now in the Smithsonian Institute, and her memoirs, cookbooks, and even letters to her husband, are all still in print.

Julia embraced the thing she loved, never became a "food snob," and continued to improve and learn until the end of her active career. She also wasn't afraid to make mistakes on the air, and requested that her mistakes not be edited out of the final version of her program. Because of this, she revolutionized cooking, and she created a cultural phenomenon.

Julia made a choice to be excellent–not perfect. That coupled with opportunity created a revolution. The next chapter will be focused on opportunities, and what to do with them.

TO RECAP:

- Excellence is ultimately doing what you love and doing it well.
- Your true self releases the anointing.
- The second part of living a life of excellence is doing what you do well.
- Little choices added to your natural talent and energized by God's anointing will result in a life of excellence.

CHAPTER ELEVEN

SAYING YES

I recently heard an interview with veteran actor Terence Stamp discussing how he took his role in *Priscilla, Queen of the Desert*. His decision was prompted by the advice of a friend who said:

"Your fear is out of proportion to the possible consequences. The only way you can find out about the fear is to keep saying 'yes.' And maybe it will go away, but if it doesn't, then you need to address your fear."[11]

Many creative people (myself included) avoid facing their fear of rejection by not taking the opportunities and open doors that become available. In practical terms, that means not saying "yes." Oscar Wilde once said "Opportunity knocks once, while temptation leans on the doorbell."

In truth, God gives us the ability to move forward in obedience.

Moving forward opens doors that get us closer to fulfilling our call. I often tell people that different choices have "juice" on them. In other words, I can sense the pleasure and the blessing of God on one choice over another. By looking for this power at work, I can

---

11 "Terence Stamp on Fellini" May 19, 2013, http://www.youtube.com/watch?v=l4RkkwrGSVg

quickly find the place that is closer to God's plan for my life. As I mentioned earlier, R.T. Kendall refers to this as the "anointing." It is the affirmation and empowerment of the Holy Spirit to help us.

We often see God's hand through the "rear view mirror." His power is made perfect in our weakness. When we look back at our lives we begin to see that we have done the impossible. We have gone beyond all that we could ask or imagine. All this happens when, in the face of fear, we say "yes."

And sadly, the opposite is also true.

In seminary I was friends with a man who came from a background of sexual brokenness. He had come through a lot of healing and transformation, and at the end of seminary was showing extraordinary ministry gifts. A well known national ministry contacted him and offered him a job preaching and teaching in the areas of sexual and relational wholeness. Out of fear, and also an awareness of his own continuing weaknesses, he turned the opportunity down. Within weeks after graduation he began to drift back into his former way of life. Today he is no longer a believer and part of the Unitarian Universalist Church.

Again and again I have seen men and women offered amazing opportunities. In fear they passed them by, and within a short time they began to be faced with intense temptations, life struggles, and difficulties that seemed to be insurmountable. There was no anointing–no supernatural ability–to overcome these difficulties. I wish it wasn't so, but there are many shipwrecked destinies that began with a simple "no."

For much of my life I have also struggled with personal brokenness. It was learning how to listen to God and do what he told me that broke the destructive patterns in my life. One of the instructions that I was given by God was "say yes to everything." In saying "yes" I often find myself in situations that need supernatural help, and I often get that help!

Every little "yes" opens doors to other opportunities. Each opportunity gives us the ability to face another fear, and every triumph gives us another testimony that reminds us that **God is with us, God is in us, and God is for us.**

INTENSE OPPORTUNITIES

The call to be a warrior artist is a call to a lifestyle that is more intense than many experience. To embrace this call requires embracing a spiritual life that is deeper and more intimate. It is not enough to make a decision to be a "Jesus follower" and then embrace much of the consumer Christianity in our world today. It means returning to the examples of our fathers and mothers in the faith, and it requires examining currently held beliefs and opinions. It means being prepared for a personal and corporate reformation. God is looking for holy people. As an artist God is calling you to use your craft–as a painter, dancer, writer, designer, film maker or musician–and create holy things.

> **God works from the inside out, and you, Artist, also create from the inside out.**

There is no hiding the movements of your soul when you are a public person. Every artist has made the choice to become a public person, because you are inviting others to see and interact with your life's work. This is why, I believe, so many artists are gripped with fear. The opportunities for rejection are almost infinite, and this is scary. In the hundreds of conversations I have had with artists, this fear of rejection prevents many from walking into their destiny.

The next move of God is going to confront arguments, ideas, and strongholds in many places. Saying "yes" to every opportunity will probably cause you to be in situations and circumstances you would NEVER have chosen. Saying yes is the way you find yourself in the right place at the right time. It is also the way you develop favor with God and with people. Excellence in all things will cause others to take notice of you, remember you, and open more opportunities for you. It was excellence that gave Daniel and his companions favor with the Babylonian Court.

Throughout his life Daniel faced the choice to sell out and succumb to the pressure to eat from the king's table, bow down to the idol the king made, and finally to worship the king as a god. Each time he refused, but at the same time, he said "yes" to the opportunities made available to him. Each time the miracles Daniel experienced increased. This gradual increase reflected the choices he made continuously over his lifetime. He chose to say "yes," to continue his ordered prayer life, and to honor those around him.

As with excellence, learning to say "yes" is made up of many little choices. I have learned as I have developed the skill of saying "yes," that two things happen:

> **I give up control, and often unintended blessings come my way.**

Really what I am talking about is the difference between wealth and poverty. Poverty has very little to do with limited resources or cash flow. Poverty is limited vision or possibilities. It is the difference between seeing the glass half full or half empty. A person gripped with a poverty mindset will turn down a job because it is not their dream position. They will not consider that a job might be a stepping stone to another opportunity, or that the job might open up relationships and possibilities in the future. Poverty is always limited. It always assumes that resources are limited and that there isn't enough to go around.

Saying "yes" will break poverty in your life like no other discipline. It will also begin to change your attitude from being negative to being positive. I am often amazed how saying "yes" to one small thing will begin to release other possibilities.

TO RECAP:
- Saying "yes" forces us to face our fear.
- God moves us forward when we say "yes."
- Saying "yes" allows us to give up control and allows unexpected blessings to come our way.
- Saying "yes" breaks the power of poverty in our lives.

CHAPTER TWELVE

LEARNING TO LISTEN: THE VOICE OF THE SHEPHERD

As I mentioned earlier, for a season I directed a crisis pregnancy center in Boston. The most rewarding part of the job was going to churches and speaking to small groups. Periodically I would be asked to speak to young people. At first I wasn't sure how to handle the issue of abortion, and sexual activity, with groups of teen and pre-teen aged kids. I began giving each student a 3x5 card and asked them to give me a question I promised that I would answer every question honestly. The index card exercise kept the groups engaged, and opened up some interesting discussions.

To my surprise the most often asked question was,
"How do I listen to God?"

Learning to listen to God is a life and death matter when you are on the front line of a move of God. Since you are called to communicate clearly, you need to know the Lord's direction, and you need to learn to discern His voice above all others. I am going to attempt to cover how I listen to God in this chapter, although many books have been written on the subject.

Listening to God is like chess. The basics are simple, but it can take a life time to become a master at hearing the Voice.

RECOGNIZING THE SHEPHERD

Jesus told us: "My sheep hear my voice, and I know them, and they follow me." (John 10:27 RSV) We have the assurance that if we are in a relationship we will be able to hear and discern the voice of Jesus. So, as I have said before, the first step is being in a relationship with God. After this you need to begin to recognize the sound of the Shepherd's voice.

In other words, you cannot begin to hear God until you first learn how God has spoken in the past, and the best way to do this is through an orderly reading of the Bible. The Bible is the record of how God has interacted with men and women over many centuries, and there are consistent patterns in these interactions. God is relational, and his communication is personal.

When I was young my devotional life was very inconsistent. Because I am highly creative, I am also highly emotional, and my imagination is usually going at a pretty rapid pace. If I depend on my feelings to guide my time with God, I find I am in the "dumps" one day, and on the "mountain top" the next day. All of this changed when I discovered the Liturgy of the Hours that were developed by the monastic communities. In the early 1990's I began a very systematic reading of the scripture–most of the psalms in a month, and the entire Bible in a year. Some parts of the Bible, like the Acts of the Apostles and the Gospels, are repeated several times throughout the year. What this type of prayer and Bible reading did for me was to create a place where I could hang my creativity.

Now you might think "that will just turn into rote repetition after a while." Yes, actually, there are some things that have become automatic. I can repeat a lot of the psalms from memory. I also have started to associate times of the year with the Bible passages assigned to that season.

Another way to look at this is to think about addiction. We know that when a person gets addicted, the brain creates mental pathways that make the behavior a repeated habit. As the addicted person repeats the negative behavior, it becomes more and more ingrained, and more and more difficult to change.

The same thing is true with the Bible. If you continue to get into the Bible in a disciplined way, you are eventually going to build pathways that create "runways" for the voice of God. You will begin to learn the way God speaks at a deep level. Jesus told us that His sheep recognize His voice and that they will not recognize the voice of an impostor. Living in the Bible does this.

Living in the Bible also helps to transform your mind. I try to keep the Bible passages from my morning prayers in my thoughts throughout the day. Because I continue to use the model of prayer from the monastery, there are some psalms I say every day, like Psalm 91. Repeating this psalm every day before bed has forced me to meditate and contemplate some of the promises it contains: no evil will happen to me, no plague will come upon me, I will tread upon the lion and the serpent, God will deliver me, and God will answer me when I call. At some point the scripture becomes a part of you. Somehow God speaks to you, your soul is refreshed, and you are also speaking to God.

This leads me to the next point:

LIVING IN THE BIBLE OPENS THE DOOR TO GOD SPEAKING TO YOU DIRECTLY.

In 1988 I had an experience with reading the Bible that forever changed how I listened to God. Up until that point, I read the Bible in my devotional time and tried to absorb whatever nutrients my soul needed from the text. In July of 1988, I was awakened in the middle of the night and heard a voice tell me to open my Bible and begin to read. What I read was the second chapter of Ezekiel, where God calls the Prophet Ezekiel and explains the kind of ministry he would have. That night the passage of scripture seemed to "leap off the page" and became intensely personal. I realized that God was speaking to *me*. It has been 25 years, and that moment with the scripture continues to impact my work, ministry, and relationship with God.

What happened to me that night in 1988 is similar to what happened to Peter the night Jesus came to the disciples walking on the water. Jesus called to Peter, and Peter said "Lord, if it is you, bid me come to you on the water." That word to Peter was heard by all the others in the boat. It was the word of Jesus. But for Peter, it was the Word of the Lord for him, and he stepped out onto the water and came to Jesus. It was a living thing for that moment, and it had power in his life as long as he chose to trust it.

Another way that God speaks is through other people. In 1995 I was attending a conference at Wheaton College and I felt unusually drawn to an African American woman from Washington, D.C. As the week progressed, we ate several meals together. During one of the meals, she spoke to me and said, "I have a word from God for you." Then she handed me a piece of paper.

> Write the vision, make it plain upon tablets, so he who runs may read it. For still the vision awaits its time; it hastens to the end–it will not lie. If it seem slow, wait for it; it will surely come, it will not delay. (Habakkuk 2:2-3)

At the time I wasn't sure what to do with this (I did not have much experience with this kind of thing) but I took the scrap of paper and put it into my Bible. Over the next 15 years I was given Habakkuk 2:2-3 by many, many people. Now I am beginning to see that God put a vision in me and I have spent a lot of time and energy writing about it. Whenever I get discouraged about the promises I have from God, someone gives me Habakkuk 2:2-3. This is God speaking through the Bible and through people.

MEASURING WHAT YOU HEAR

Before I talk about some of the other ways God speaks, it is important to emphasize that God speaks first in the words of the Bible. Everything else I hear gets measured against the Biblical record. We can avoid a lot of problems by letting the Bible be our standard. Any time you "hear" something that is directly in conflict with the clear reading of scripture, you are heading into dangerous territory.

As I mentioned earlier, I initially pursued becoming a priest in the Episcopal Church. Although I knew it was going to be challenging, I never expected the challenges I eventually faced. Around the time that I entered the priesthood process, the chairman of the ordination committee announced to his church that he was leaving his wife and children for another woman. He claimed that God "told" him to do this on Easter Sunday while he was presiding over Holy Communion. Because of his claim that God was instructing him to do this, the denomination and his parish allowed this to continue. Because this clergyman and his denomination no longer put stock in the authority of the Bible (and quite probably were ignorant of much of it), they became deceived into believing this direction to commit adultery was from God. They were deceived into thinking that some other voice was the voice of the Shepherd.

Another mainline denomination recently ran an ad campaign with the quote "Do not put a period where God put a comma: God is still speaking." The quote was attributed to Gracie Allen, a famous comedienne from the early twentieth century. The message was clear–other voices, even those of dead Jewish entertainers, can speak to us over the clear word of the Bible.

DEVELOPING YOUR HEARING

That said, God does speak to us in other ways, because He is living. He wants to have a relationship with you built on trust and mutual, open communication. Once you begin to make the Bible a living part of you, the ability to recognize the voice of the Shepherd will increase.

Part of my daily life is taking time to wait on God. This usually involves sitting in silence, often with a notebook and pen nearby. God will "download" thoughts, ideas, and direction to me. If my mind is cluttered or I am distracted, I may take a walk or go for a drive in the car. It has been amazing over the years to see how God has given me clarity or given me answers to problems through this simple exercise.

Even as I write this book, there have been moments when I have gotten "stuck."

As an artist I have discovered that my process is often a collaboration with the Holy Spirit. For instance, I needed to take several weeks off from writing this book, after a period of writing almost one chapter a week. My break became almost six weeks, and when I got back on the job, my brain felt "clogged." My original outline called for three concluding chapters, but my ideas were not flowing. I quietly prayed, and asked God for some direction. Then I got up from the computer, went for a brisk walk, and took a shower. In the shower the Lord began speaking to me. I heard the Lord say "it's time to get practical." As I thought about all I had written, I discovered there were enough ideas for EIGHT more chapters. As you can see, listening involves you and God working together.

ELIMINATING NOISE

Of course, when I describe a voice, I am describing an inward whisper. The voice will come like a thought that somehow you didn't think yourself. Recognizing the voice of God requires beginning to practice quiet and eliminating outside "noise." This takes time, practice, and pursuit. Over the years I have tried to be a good steward of the things I hear, and have recorded them in notebooks. Over time I have learned what is God, and what is my own inner "stuff." I have also been able to recognize some of my own blind spots. We all have areas where our own soul can imitate the voice of God, and we can get off track.

Leanne Payne often talked about learning to listen to God in her Pastoral Care Ministry Schools. Many times she described teaching young college students how to listen to God. Invariably, young women would return to her and say that God told them the name of the man they were going to marry. Young men all came back and said God told them they would be the next Billy Graham!

The greatest instruction I had in listening to God was through visits to the Abbey of Our of Lady of Gethsemani in Trappist, Kentucky. The monks at Gethsemani keep a strict discipline of silence, and the countryside around the monastery is one of the quietest places on earth. My first visit was very difficult because I had a lot of interior noise. The quiet was actually upsetting, and I left after four days a little shaken by the experience. On later visits I chose to enter into the silence and found that God began speaking to me, and also healing some of my deep emotional wounds. Eventually I began to make silence a regular part of my life.

Silence is one powerful way to remove distractions. I find that periodic fasts from the news, media, internet, and entertainment are also helpful when learning to listen to God. Over the past few years media fasts have been especially cleansing, and my "hearer" becomes more able to hear the gentle voice of the Holy Spirit when the fast is over.

HEART LANGUAGE

How God speaks is more about your heart than about the method of listening. There is no one in the Universe who knows you better than the One who created you. This Father has been with you from before the creation of the world. He knows your DNA, your family history, and every thing that ever happened to you. God knows the language of your heart. Because of this, God can speak to you in a number of ways. It is a lot like when you have a long time best friend who has shared many things with you. You have secrets and "inside jokes" that almost no one else would understand without a lot of explanation. I have one friend for whom the word "cheese ball" causes us to roar with laughter. To explain why "cheese ball" is funny would take too long. But this is part of the language of the heart between me and my friend. When you begin to understand that God speaks this way, then a song you hear on the radio, a line from a movie, or even an aroma on the air can all be messages from God to you.

In one of our recent prayer meetings we spent time praying for individuals. I was playing the piano quietly, and suddenly felt the urge to play the old hymn "Like a River Glorious is God's Perfect Peace." After the prayer meeting the man receiving prayer came up to me and thanked me for playing that hymn. My friend explained that even as a child that hymn was used by God to encourage and strengthen him. Honestly, after the Bible, I believe the language of the heart is the most common way God speaks to people. As artists, we need to be tuned in, because God may be speaking even when we are not aware–and he might be using us!

GOOD RECEPTION

After getting into the scripture, learning to wait on God, and learning the language of the heart, it is critical that you keep your "receptors" clean. Oswald Chambers, the author of *My Utmost for His Highest* described developing a Holy Imagination.

Our imagination is one of the most important parts of our mind. It gives us the ability to see the impossible. It helps us see the unseen. Through our imagination we are given the opportunity to be creative. This is something that reflects the personality of God more than anything else.

Our imaginations are so important that the enemy of our souls in this day has made it a major battleground for the destruction of humanity. At no other time in history has it been possible to access visual images, sounds, music, or material that is negative or defiling to the imagination. Pornography and violence probably do more damage to the imagination than anything else. Both of these things become limits on the soul.

The holy imagination becomes a place where God can interface with us. When we have a cleansed imagination, we can hear the things God tells us about ourselves, about the world, and about Himself, and we can freely receive. Not only that, but we also begin to discover that nothing is impossible with God. Our wildest imaginations can become reality. There are no limits to what God can do if we yield ourselves to him. The Bible talks about taking every thought captive to the will of God. This is how we maintain our imaginations. Paul tells us "no eye has seen, no ear has heard, and no mind has ever conceived the glorious things that God has prepared for those who have believed" (I Corinthians 2:9). If you feel you have defiled your imagination, you can pray the following prayer:

Lord Jesus, I have looked on things that are unholy, and I have been defiled by them. I know that my imagination is the platform you use to change me, and to change the world. I give my imagination to you, and I ask you, by the power of the Holy Spirit, to cleanse the imaginations of my heart.

(If images begin to appear, take your hand, and pull them out of your thoughts, keep doing this until no more appear.)

Thank you for healing my imagination. Help me
to hear, see, and do what you want me to do. Fill
my imagination with a sense of the holy, the good,
and the beautiful, in Jesus name. Amen.

In our next chapter we are going to continue talking about listening to God through the prophetic and through the seer anointing.

TO RECAP:

- Learning to listen to God is a life and death matter when you are on the front line of a move of God.
- The Bible is the best way to learn how God has spoken in the past.
- Spending time in the Bible develops the ability to hear God directly.
- The Bible is the standard for all things we hear from God.
- Once you begin to make the Bible a living part of you, the ability to recognize the voice of the Shepherd will increase.
- Recognizing the voice of God requires beginning to practice quiet and eliminating outside "noise."
- God knows the language of your heart.
- We need to keep our ability to hear clean.

CHAPTER THIRTEEN

LEARNING TO LISTEN:
THE CREATIVE PROPHET

After discovering how to listen to God for yourself, it will not be unusual for you to begin listening to God for others. In biblical language, we call this the prophetic. A simple definition for the prophetic is God speaking to a person through another person. In other words, God uses people to minister his Person, Power and Presence. God uses people to speak his words to others.

My guess is, if you are a gifted artist, you have the gift of prophecy at some level.

The Holy Spirit is the giver of all gifts, and out of His indwelling Presence you can operate in the prophetic. There are different types of prophetic gifting, but they all are rooted in the basic reality that God is always speaking, and the art of listening will help us hear what God is saying to us and to others.

The nature of art is to reveal and communicate. Over many years of working with both artists and prophets, I have seen many common struggles in the two groups.

They both struggle with being misunderstood by others. Usually creative people are seeing possibilities and seeing what exists in their highly developed imaginations. Prophets often see things in the future. The average conventional person, on the other hand, only sees and understands things as they are. This is the reason why so many gifted artists have difficulty finding a platform or an audience. It is also why many prophets are martyred in their own generation, and then revered after their death. It is also why many biblical prophecies get misinterpreted. All of this can sometimes result in an immobilizing fear of rejection that prevents the artist and the prophet from taking risks.

Prophets and artists both tend to run ahead of the crowd. There is a good reason why the Bible refers to "forerunners." The prophets and the artists often catch a glimpse of what is just beyond the horizon. They also both tend to be pioneers that create a "new normal" that others follow and often take for granted. It's amazing how new artistic movements, like the innovations in music and art in the 20th Century, were greeted with the same kinds of angry mobs and protests that several old testament prophets faced. Today we look back at jazz, rock and roll, and modern dance, and see how these have become the back drop of the larger culture, even though they were hated at first.

They both tend to be the first to see what's missing or what is wrong with an object or situation. Pablo Picasso once said that "the first act of creation is an act of destruction." I think what he meant is something I have seen in my own life. If something is aesthetically out of place or missing (especially in a church building during the sermon) I find myself fixated on how to correct the visual problem. A prophet does the same thing–they become fixated on the thing that is out of line with God's word. It may be the toleration of idols, the disobedience to the command to rebuild the temple, or moral corruption. The prophet speaks to the thing that is broken and gives the remedy. Of course, when a person lacks maturity, this expresses itself in being overly critical. A person can become a church critic or an art critic but never actually create a better ministry or a work of art.

Artists and prophets both tend to have dramatic highs and lows. One needs only to look at the lives of Jonah, Jeremiah, Elijah, Paul, and John the Baptist to see how one moment a prophet can be ecstatic in the power of the Spirit, and then suddenly want to end his life. Creativity often comes with a rush of emotion that brings a real "high" then is followed by deep exhaustion, depression, and the feeling of being "poured out like a drink offering." This cycle has been seen in the lives of many artists, including Michelangelo and Vincent Van Gogh. Even some of the great preachers, most notably Martin Luther (who was a prophet and an artist) suffered from dramatic highs and lows. We all know stories of artists who ended their lives too soon because they couldn't navigate the low.

Artists and prophets are often deeply sensitive people. This sensitivity helps the creative and prophetic person to hear and see new things, and respond to a lot of different stimuli at once. At the same time, because of the tendency to experience rejection, be misunderstood by others, or be ahead of the crowd, the creative/prophetic person may develop a "hard edge." This is especially strong in creative professions where there is a lot of competition. People can become very nasty to others who are in the same field. In the church prophets can respond to the hurt they experience by pulling back from relationships, floating from one church to another, or becoming negative toward leaders and leadership. It is not uncommon for both prophetic and creative people to deal with their pain through addictive patterns—sex, drugs, alcohol, or self destruction.

I believe that even if someone is not a believer, God can still "program" someone with an innate prophetic gifting. Because they were not believers, this gifting often gets manifested in destructive ways. In some cases (not all) the artist chooses to embrace demonic forces and use their gifts for evil. Pablo Picasso, Henri Matisse, Elvis, Madonna, and the Beatles all pushed the boundaries for art and music in the last century. After each of these artists hit the scene, people never looked at things the way they did before. In this sense they all functioned as prophets. It is clear when looking at artistic movements over the past 100 years, that some of these men and women willingly embraced evil spiritual forces to advance their careers.

SEEING THE UNSEEN

Of the ways God communicates, the Seer gift is especially key to the Prophetic Artist. Beyond words and thoughts, the Seer gift opens up the realm of creativity. James Goll has said "Not all prophets are seers, but all seers are prophets." [12] The term comes from the Hebrew word "Naʿ bi." This was the earliest word used for prophet in the Bible, and it literally means "seer."

How this gift functions is very interesting. There is a two-fold aspect to the seer anointing.

Often if someone is operating in the seer gifting, they will begin to see things "in the spirit." This may be a strong mental picture or image. It may also be a sound, or even a smell. For example, in my ministry in Salem, I will often be walking through the city and smell an odor that I call "putrescence." It is a mixture of rotting flesh and sewage, and it is present whenever there is witchcraft in

---

12 Goll, James W., "The Prophetic Power of the Seer," September 25, 2004, elijahlist.com

operation. I have also smelled incense, and roses during times of prayer. It is not uncommon for me to pray for a person and see an image, like chains around their heart. I can then use the visual image to guide my prayer. It is also not uncommon for artists or worship leaders to hear musical tunes or see colors. These are all ways that the seer anointing can function.

The second aspect of the seer anointing is the lifestyle aspect. It is not uncommon for a seer to run two or more years ahead of the crowd. God might ask you to so something and you do it in obedience. This is truly a forerunner ministry for the larger Body of Christ. Just when others start embracing this reality, God will probably move you on to something else.

When I was in my mid-thirties, I reached a period where I was really tired of being misunderstood by my church leadership. It seemed I was always getting into trouble for being "insubordinate" for following God's leading, only to see my church embrace whatever I was doing about two years later. Sadly, I wasn't being rebellious or trying to make trouble (in fact, I was struggling hard to be supportive of my church leadership). It was my spiritual mom in the prophetic, Sharen Cook, who explained what was happening.

"You are walking in the prophetic," she said, "and God has you running ahead of the pack. Don't fight it, embrace it." When I understood what God was doing in my life, I learned to actually rest in it. As I made peace with this lifestyle, I had fewer conflicts with those in my life who were threatened by my gifting.

PENNIES FROM HEAVEN

Another piece of the seer lifestyle is how God will speak through random events, movements, or objects. Sometimes I will recognize patterns.

About 8 years ago I began finding pennies all over the place. I would stop to get gas and find a penny on the pump handle. I would go to a restaurant and find a penny leaning on its side against the salt shaker, and most common of all, I would open my car door and find a penny on the ground. It happened so often that I almost became obsessed with what it could mean.

Eventually, with some help, I figured out that it was about my identity in ministry. Usually the pennies were tail side up, where it says "ONE CENT." This was a play on words–I am a "Sent One." Amazingly, after I figured it out, I realized I was finding pennies when I was unsure of my calling or mission. The pennies were little reminders that I was being sent.

Later on I began finding dimes, and that was also an interesting message. "ONE DIME" was also a play on words. When ever I find a dime I know I am "on time"–I am in the right place at the right time.

What I have learned over the years is that God is always speaking, and He understands the language of your heart. God wants to have an intimate relationship with you that is precious. There are things that will mean something of importance to only you and God. It is amazing how once you get "tuned in" you begin to see God speaking to you through movies, books, signs on the road, music in the mall, and random things you find on the sidewalk. This kind of relationship then can enrich you and give you the ability to communicate to others.

Taking this to the next level, God will then begin to use the prophetic gifting through your art. For me personally, I am seeing God touch people through my paintings. Sometimes people will see things I didn't intend to paint. In one case I know of a woman who was freed from clinical depression as she watched me paint. I am not sure how God did this, but I am thankful! Seeing how the Holy Spirit has begun speaking to others through my artwork has freed me to take risks and allow God to guide me in the creative process. It has become a fun adventure.

If you are sensing that you may be functioning in the prophetic at some level, I encourage you to begin keeping a record of how this gift is operating in your life. If you are a visual artist, keep a photographic record and a record of testimonies related to your paintings. If you are musician try to record as much as you can. It is also critical to keep in relationship with others who understand your unique gifting and can keep you accountable. I think being in a church that has "grid" for the prophetic can be very helpful. Fortunately there are many ministries and organizations today who can help you grow in maturity in this area. At the end of this book I will have a list of resources that can help you grow and develop as a seer, a prophet, and an artist.

In the next chapter we will talk about the core of the life of a warrior artist, developing a lifestyle of worship.

TO RECAP:

- The prophetic is God speaking to a person through another person.
- Artists are often prophets.
- Creative people and prophetic people have similar struggles and characteristics.
- The Seer gift opens up the realm of creativity.
- A Seer expresses their gift through "seeing" or through lifestyle.

CHAPTER FOURTEEN

LIVING A LIFE OF WORSHIP

Eight years ago God gave me some clear direction: "Worship in the morning and write in the afternoon." As often is the case, the Lord will direct you to do something and the end result will be something completely unexpected. The fifteen minutes of singing at the piano in the morning has grown into as many as twenty hours a week in various houses of prayer, and numerous songs that were composed in these worship sessions.

A major turning point for me in leading worship was taking the "hymns" from the Book of Revelation and printing them out. These are the passages in Revelation that are arranged in poetic form and interrupt the narrative at times. It begins to become clear that Revelation is really arranged like a musical, with much of the action being moved along by songs from Heaven. One day I attempted to sing some of these songs in our prayer sets. We began with Revelation 4:11:

You are worthy, our Lord and God, to receive glory and honor and power, for you created all things, and by your will they were created and have their being.

That first song seemed to never end. We sang it for over 3 hours! That experience began to revolutionize my understanding of what worship is and what our call as artists is in this moment.

As I stated earlier, God is raising up an army of artisans. In the study that began this book, a common thread can be found with the artisan in scripture. In Exodus they were called to build the place of worship. As we know, that place was created to be a visual representation of the revelation of heaven that Moses experienced.

If you are going to be a warrior artist, and carry the Presence, Power, and Person of God, you are required to live a life of worship. Worship is the common thread through every chapter of this book.

Worship is not about what happens for one hour on Sunday. Sadly, what is often called a "worship service" is really either some form of entertainment with a religious theme or a musical program with a lecture. As Bill Johnson said in a recent sermon, "Much of church is people coming to see who else is at the party but never talking to the host." Church is often focused on the horizontal aspect of life, and church services often are rated by "what did I get out of it."

In contrast, true worship is about the vertical relationship. It is about meeting the Host and serving, blessing, and adoring Him. I think what hit me when we began singing out of Revelation is that we suddenly aligned with heaven. Heaven is about the Lamb who is at the center of the throne. For all time and eternity, there is a company singing "Worthy is the Lamb who was slain, to receive power, wealth, wisdom and strength, honor and glory and praise!" (Revelation 5:12).

AGAINST THE CURRENT

Living a life of worship is counter-cultural. It isn't about you. It's not about your gift, your ministry, your calling, or your career. It's about HIM. This distinction is what sets the army of artists apart. If you are called to this company, then you are called to a radical proposition–the call to live a life of worship.

> I appeal to you therefore, by the mercies of God, to present your bodies as a living sacrifice, holy and acceptable to God, which is your spiritual act of worship. Do not be conformed to this world, but be transformed by the renewal of your mind, that you may prove what is the will of God, what is good and acceptable and perfect. (Romans 12:1-2)

Let's unpack this verse a little.

Worship involves your body. Earlier in the book we talked a lot about the Incarnation and the means of grace. As an artist you are also called to create things that God can use. God loves physical things. God loves your body. God loves the created order. Many Christians think they can be more spiritual than Jesus. They seem to forget that Jesus touched dirty people. The Bible even tells us that Jesus needed to get his feet washed, and that he needed to eat. Jesus had a physical body, and when he returns it will be in a physical body.

Worship begins when you say, "Jesus here is my body, I offer it to you as a living sacrifice." In short, that means the Holy Spirit can fill your body, and use it. Your body is the vehicle for the kingdom of heaven to use. That means that how you treat your body, and what you do with it matters to God.

There is a positive and a negative side to this. You get to enjoy all kinds of good things with your body–smells, taste, touch, the Presence of the Holy Spirit. You get to go places and do things that please and bless God. But you also can't use your body for things that will hurt it. You can't indulge in sexual activity that is outside God's design. You have to learn to be a steward of the body God gave you because it is good, and it belongs to God as a vessel of worship. In another place Paul tells us that the body is the temple of the Holy Spirit. (II Corinthians 6:16) It is this place that is center of worship, and all other "worship" flows out of this worship center.

Worship is a living sacrifice. In Exodus 23:15 there is an overlooked phrase: "None shall appear before me empty-handed." When I first came to New England I was a little shocked at how often a church gathering was held without making an offering. I asked the Lord about this, and sensed strongly that making an offering would help bring the breakthrough to the region. A few times I was given the opportunity to share this, and we had an offering. I was stunned at how many people refused to give for whatever reason.

All real worship requires that you make a sacrifice. In the place of the finest of the flock, Jesus himself offered his Body as the perfect sacrifice. Daily we are called to join our bodies to his offering. This means making small excellent choices of obedience to his call on our lives. It means saying "yes" when we would rather say no, and it means being inconvenienced at times. This is the practical part of embracing the Cross of Christ. It is saying "not my will, but yours."

Worship does not conform you to the world. In an average week I lead 8 hours of worship. As I stated earlier, my style of worship is very "vertical." I emphasize recreating the sounds of heaven, and use the lyrics of heaven– scripture–as much as possible. Sometimes a person unfamiliar with my ministry will join us. If they are accustomed to a lot of the commercial worship music being sung in church they sometimes visibly react to what's happening. I have seen people "shut down" as the worship set goes on. In recent months as the "quiet revival" in New England gets less quiet, more and more people are responding to this vertical worship and entering in. My style didn't change, the hunger for heaven in people did.

True worship is not about how you feel. It is not about what makes you happy. Real worship will run counter to American culture that is consumed with how you feel and how happy you are.

Early in my time worshiping at home I found myself stuck and bored. A strange thought crossed my mind. "God, what do you want me to sing? Which song do you want to hear?" It had never occurred to me that God might have an opinion on what I was singing.

I do a lot of consulting with churches in the area of worship and prayer. Often I find that contemporary worship songs tend to be focused on a person's experience with God, or their feelings about God, and not God. Once I was working with a worship leader and I suggested he could improve his worship sets by going through his collection and removing all of the songs that began with the word "I." He was stunned when he went home and found about 50 songs in his repertoire that began this way.

When I lead worship, I focus on heaven and the sounds of heaven. Over many years I have discovered that if you go "up" first, and focus on the Ultimate you can come down and focus on the intimate. These sets always end with the congregation in a strong sense of rest and peace. When you start low, and focus on the intimate, you never get intimate. I do the same thing when I paint. I try to ask God to reveal to me something about Himself that can be communicated to others.

Worship transforms you. Living a life of worship is going to impact every area of your life. We have been singing out of the book of Revelation for almost three years. Often you will find phrases like "You are worthy to receive wealth, power, honor, and might." I wondered about this for a while. How can we give wealth to someone who created all things? How can we give power to someone who is all powerful?

I pondered this for sometime, and finally asked the Lord to give me understanding. I was a little surprised when the Lord spoke to me and said that when we ascribe these things to him, he is able to pour them out on us. It becomes a divine exchange of grace.

We become like the thing we worship. Psalm 115 describes the idols that pagan nations worship. They have eyes but are blind. They have ears but are deaf. The idols have mouths, but cannot speak. Then it says, so are the people who make them. They have become increasingly blind, dumb, and deaf. By contrast, the more time you spend with God in worship the more you become like him–loving, kind, gentle, gracious. You become like the thing you look upon.

Obviously you can see the correlation between this truth and the other truths we have discussed. The life of worship cleanses the imagination. The life of worship releases creativity and fresh ideas. Nothing will impact the nature and character of the creative life than a commitment to live as a worshiper.

A life of worship is the best argument that you are doing the perfect will of God.

Saint Francis famously said, "preach the Gospel at all times, and if necessary, use words."

Living a life of worship will come through your art. You can't hide what's happening on the inside. If you are giving your body to God as a temple, and you are spending time with him; then others will begin to notice.

Of course, worship is more than singing songs. Personally, I believe there are four components to living a life of worship that are essential. If you make these things a habit, everything else is details.

1. You have to give generously. Ten percent tithing is the minimum. God is generous, and you need to follow his example. I find the Lord is always stretching me in the area of giving.

2. You need to commit to verbally worshiping God. What comes out of your mouth can stimulate your faith. I discipline myself to make sure the first words out of my mouth when I awake in the morning are words of worship. This morning I began by saying "Holy, Holy, Holy." I encourage you to read the psalms out loud. I use a prayer book that has pages and pages of ancient songs from the church like the *Te Deum* and the *Gloria in Excelsis Deo.* I am a singer, so I do spend a lot of time in song throughout the day. This is an excellent way to worship.

3. You need to receive Holy Communion often. Holy Communion is many things, but at its center is the perfect act of worship that Jesus offered the Father. When we come to receive Holy Communion, we are participating in the Body and Blood of the Lord. We are proclaiming his death until he comes again. By the Holy Spirit we are being fed and empowered to be broken bread and poured out wine for the life of the world.

4. You need to be obedient to the Lord's direction. As I have said earlier, listening to the Lord and doing what he told me was what transformed my life. The most ultimate act of worship is joyful obedience to the Holy Spirit, saying "Yes Lord, not my will but yours."

All real kingdom warriors are worshipers. You artist, are called to live a life that reflects Jesus himself. Every act of creation is designed to be an act of worship where you glorify God and enjoy Him forever. It is the highest calling and commission in creation.

> *Te Deum*
> *We praise you O God:*
> *We acclaim you as the Lord;*
> *All creation worships you,*
> *the Father everlasting.*
> *To you all angels, all the powers of heaven:*
> *the cherubim and seraphim sing in endless praise,*
> *Holy, Holy, Holy, Lord! God of power and might.*
> *Heaven and earth are full of your glory.*
> *The glorious company of apostles praise you.*
> *The noble fellowship of prophets praise you.*
> *The white robed army of martyrs praise you.*
> *Throughout the world, the Holy Church acclaims you.*
> *Father, of majesty unbounded;*
> *Your true and only Son, worthy of all praise;*
> *the Holy Spirit, Advocate and Guide.*
> *You, Christ, are the King of Glory:*

the eternal Son of the Father.
When you took our flesh to set us free,
You humbly chose the Virgin's womb.
You overcame the sting of death,
and opened the kingdom of heaven to all believers.
You are seated at God's right hand in glory;
and we believe you will come to be our judge.
Come then Lord, and help your people,
bought with the price of your own blood,
and bring us with all your saints,
into glory everlasting. Amen.

Gloria in Excelsis Deo
Glory to God in the highest
and peace to his people on earth.
Lord God, heavenly King, almighty God and Father,
we worship you, we give you thanks,
we praise you for your glory.
Lord Jesus Christ, only Son of the Father,
Lord God, Lamb of God,
you take away the sin of the world,
have mercy on us.
You are seated at the right hand of the Father:
receive our prayer.
For you alone are the Holy One,
you alone are the Lord,
you alone are the Most High, Jesus Christ,
with the Holy Spirit,
in the glory of God the Father. Amen.

TO RECAP:

- Warrior artists are required to live a life of worship.
- Living a life of worship is counter-cultural.
- Worship involves your body.
- Worship is a living sacrifice.
- Worship does not conform you to the world.
- Worship transforms you.
- A life of worship is the best argument that you are doing the perfect will of God.

CHAPTER FIFTEEN

REST

---

*For thus says the Lord God, the Holy One of Israel, "In returning
and rest you shall be saved; in quietness and in trust shall be your
strength."*
(Isaiah 30:15)

In the first part of *An Army Arising* I mentioned that the call to
Oholiab and Bezalel in Exodus came in the same chapter that
God gave Moses the command to institute the Sabbath. Rest and
Creativity are eternally joined.

In contrast, I would say nothing marks this current age more
profoundly than restlessness. We have 24/7 grocery shops, the
busiest day in the week for all retailers is Sunday and the stream
of media never seems to end. Because many of us in the church
are part of this culture, church activity and "ministry" also never
seem to end. If you are freelance artist, you also know the constant
pressure that having a non- structured life can bring. There are
many nights when I have fallen into bed wondering if I have done
enough, worked hard enough, or reached my set goals for the day.

The warrior artist requires a discipline of rest. I believe there are
three kinds of rest presented to us in scripture–the daily rest of
sleep, the weekly rest from labor, and the spiritual rest from anxiety
and striving.

THE ENEMIES OF REST

We need to begin by talking about the enemies of rest. Before going any further it is important to state that even if your work is not physical, it is still work. Mental work and spiritual work are just as taxing, and in some cases more taxing, than physical labor. This is a double "whammy" because often it is more difficult to measure the outcome of your efforts.

As I have mentioned throughout this book, I lead many hours of prayer meetings each week. One day a dear friend came to visit one of the meetings. A few days later she commented to me "Wow, prayer really tires you out!"

A major enemy of rest is the demonic notion of the starving artist. Every artist I know has been asked at least once "Why don't you get a real job?" Conventional people undervalue the work of creative people (even though they depend on it).[13] Because the arts and creative activity are seen as less valuable, many artists work twice as hard to prove that they have a "real job." Being a creative professional is about as difficult a job as you can have–you are part entrepreneur, part self-employed, and part public personality. This is beyond any job in an office, factory, or cubicle, and it requires a deeper level of rest.

Another enemy of rest is a misunderstanding of the creative work cycle. It has taken me many years to recognize how my process works. After many discussions with other artists, I have learned that most creative people have a cycle they work through as they create.

---

13 To understand the difference between conventional and creative people I highly recommend Carol Eikleberry's book, *The Career Guide for Creative and Unconventional People*, Berkeley, CA:Ten Speed Press, 2007.

A project begins with an idea. The idea may come with initial excitement. For instance, I had a sense for several months that I needed to write a book that summarized all that I have learned over the past seven years with Belonging House. That initial excitement was birthed out of a Bible study on the artist in scripture. I sketched out an outline. Then I set a goal that I would write one chapter a week beginning in January. The first few weeks were great, but then I began to lose excitement and energy. My ideas stopped flowing, and I needed to set the book aside. I spent several weeks going over where I was in the process (I should also add I had significant amount of guilt that I didn't meet my goal of one chapter a week).

I would describe the time when I wasn't producing chapters an "incubation period." My ideas needed to be sorted out. Even though there wasn't a measurable product, I was still working on the book.

In mid-March I returned to my one chapter a week schedule, and kept at this for a season. I should also mention that the book was being published live on www.Leanpub.com. Because of this, my readers were giving me feedback. This feedback helped me recognize that I was taking the book in the wrong direction. I stopped writing again and actually took down a whole section of the book and did major rewrites, and then needed another "incubation period" before I began writing again. This cycle has repeated now about three times–a season of productivity followed by a season of dormancy, followed by a season of greater clarity and creativity that leads back into productivity.

The entire process has been work, even though at times it would appear to my readers that I am not doing anything.

Understanding the cycle will help you grasp that you need to rest, and in resting you will begin to experience greater creativity.

THE DAILY REST OF SLEEP.

There have been several studies in recent years about the relationship between rest and creativity. Although there is not enough scientific evidence to say artists need more sleep (there wasn't one study I felt confident about quoting in this section), there is lots of anecdotal evidence that sleep impacts your creative life. I am more creative if I can get 8 hours of sleep a night. After periods of extensive creative output (like a week of leading prayer, speaking, and then painting at a conference–while writing a book) I have found myself sleeping up to 12 hours at a time.

During times of heavy activity I will also steal a 20 minute nap. These "cat naps" do wonders for my creativity.

Years ago I developed the habit of praying the monastic office of Compline before bed. These prayers are centered around several Psalms. Compline has done wonders in improving my quality of sleep. I have also tried to get to bed early and wake up naturally. This process has allowed sleep to truly become a recovery period every day. Over time I have seen how God speaks to me early as I am just beginning to wake up. As Psalm 172:2 tells us, God gives his beloved sleep.

THE WEEKLY REST FROM LABOR

There are many principles in scripture that I believe are universal principles, almost like the laws of nature. One of these is the concept of *sabbath*. God chose one day out of the week and rested. In college I first made the decision to take one day and walk away from my studies at the advice of my spiritual father George Wells. I discovered that my grades improved, even though my time in study decreased.

Over the years I have discovered a surprising truth in taking a sabbath. A sabbath forces you to let go of what ever you are working on, no matter how important, and release it to God. Once a week you get a gentle reminder that the work does not own you. You are also forced to let go of control, and trust God that it will get finished.

Truthfully, I have sometimes found that the sabbath day ends with me feeling more tired than I expected. Because I have intentionally interrupted the daily grind, I sometimes feel a little off center. But, the time of rest is especially apparent to those who are involved in my work. After getting rest I find I am sharper, more creative, and better able to handle the many surprises that life seems to bring.

THE SPIRITUAL REST FROM ANXIETY AND STRIVING

The book of Hebrews puts it this way: "So then, there remains a sabbath rest for the people of God; for whoever enters God's rest also ceases from his labors as God did from his." (Hebrews 4:9-10 RSV).

The rest described here is not a day off, but a shift that has occurred because Jesus Christ finished the work on the cross. Hebrews tells us that Jesus is seated at the right hand of the Father. He is no longer working to offer sacrifices because his one sacrifice was enough to put an end to sin and death.

My friend Myles Milham recently shared with me an encounter he had where God began revealing to him the power of the cross of Christ. Myles described to me what looked like tentacles that were wrapped around the earth, and these tentacles held the earth in a tight grip. What he was seeing was the power of sin that held the earth. Then the Lord revealed the power of the cross and blood of Jesus that came like an axe and cut through these tentacles and they released the earth. It was clear from what Myles saw that we have not grasped how deeply and completely Jesus has freed us from the curse of sin.

All the other forms of rest emerge out of the core sense of rest that comes when you experience the reality that Jesus completed the work for you on the cross. No human works can make God like you, make God happy, or give you right standing with God. Jesus completely made peace with God, so that you can enter that rest. Earlier in this book I shared the lists of promises given to us because Jesus really lives in us. These promises are all part of God's rest that is available to you.

This might be a good time for you take a break from reading and ask God to give you a revelation of his rest. When I find myself caught up in anxious striving, I put my hand on my heart and pray this prayer:

Jesus, I know that I am in you, and you are in me. I believe that you are in the Father, and because of this, the Father is in me. I am in you, you are in me. Thank you.

I then take a deep breath and pause. It's amazing how this little exercise gets me back in touch with the Presence of God in me, and also gets me realigned with God's rest. My perfectionism and anxious striving usually go away.

IT'S OKAY TO HAVE FUN

A few months ago a dear friend gave me a little gift bag. I dumped it out on my desk and found an interesting collection:

> several sheets of colored paper
> about a dozen crayons
> a bottle of bubble soap
> stickers
> candy
> some false teeth
> seashells
> a rubber ball
> a bunch of colored pens
> a bouncy ball
> balloons

Obviously, my friend thought I was taking myself a little too seriously.

The other side of rest is fun. God wants to have fun with us, and taking rest is part of the process. As an artist you have permission to have fun with God, and to take time off. I mean, think about it, God wants to raise up an army of people who sing, dance, paint, tell stories, and do a bunch of other fun things. Getting rest, taking a break, and having fun are all powerful weapons in our arsenal if we are part of the Army Arising.

TO RECAP:

- All warrior artists need a discipline of rest.
- Even if your work is not physical, it is still work.
- You need the daily rest of sleep, the weekly rest from labor, and the spiritual rest from anxiety and striving.
- It is okay to have fun.

CHAPTER SIXTEEN

TAKING YOUR PLACE AT THE GATE

About ten years ago I was invited to attend a small leaders gathering with Os Guinness. Guinness remarked that in the United States more than 25% of the population considers themselves Evangelical Christian. At the same time, roughly 2% of the population is Jewish. (2012 statistics indicate there are 6 million Jews in the United States, just under 14 million worldwide.) Although the Evangelical community is a fairly large group in the United States, remarked Guinness, their influence and role in public life seems to be continuously declining. By contrast, the Jewish community has a huge impact on society and culture. The difference that Guinness pointed out was "Jews take their place at the gate."

What he was describing was the example set by Mordecai in the Biblical book of Esther.

Mordecai, Esther's uncle, sat at the city gate in Babylon and paid attention to all that was happening in the city. He was the first to hear the news, and when possible he even influenced the events he heard about. Because of his strategic location, Mordecai foiled a plot to assassinate the the king, and this eventually led to Esther saving the entire Jewish people from genocide. This story, and the example of Mordecai, are retold and re-enacted each year during the Jewish festival of Purim.

Taking a seat at the gate has been a part of Jewish survival ever since the Babylonian Captivity. The influence of this tiny minority group is staggering. Currently three U.S. Supreme Court justices are Jewish. The top three most powerful men in Hollywood, Jeffrey Katzenberg, Stephen Spielberg, and David Geffen are Jewish. Throughout the past 500 hundred years, Jews have disproportionately been represented in banking, commerce, education and science. This trend is so strong that anti-semitic conspiracy theories resurface periodically. Pretty amazing for less than 5% of current world population.

By contrast, in the United States roughly 40% of the population attends church weekly, and 75% consider themselves Christian. (I found these statistics on Wikipedia.) As stated earlier, about 26.9% consider themselves Evangelical. Around the time that I sat across from Os Guinness, a majority of Christian ministries were moving out of New York City and Los Angeles. Most of these moved to Colorado Springs, Colorado. Many others moved to Orlando, Florida. It is not surprising that after Christians gave up their place in the geographic centers of influence huge shifts began to happen in film, television, music, journalism, and now government. Although Christians still command an extraordinary majority in the United States, many feel they are a persecuted minority.

INFLUENCE WHEN YOU NEED IT

I moved to Boston in 2008, not long after same-sex marriage was legalized in the state. As I talked to the many discouraged men and women who tried to prevent this law from passing, an interesting picture emerged. Many Christians lamented that gay lobbyists had "infiltrated" the Massachusetts State House, and for years had been volunteering in the offices of elected officials. They were making copies, stuffing envelopes, and shredding papers. One day, after hearing these complaints in a meeting, I spoke up.

"Jesus told us the greatest would be the one who serves, and the gay community chose to serve. In taking this place, they gained a place of influence. When the gay marriage vote happened, many of those who voted for gay marriage had a name and face connected to their vote. They had met someone for whom their vote mattered."

The place at the gate will give you influence in the moment you need it.

RADICAL RETHINKING

At the beginning of this book I stated that this is the moment when the war is about ideas, and this is the moment of the story. We are being called to a radical reformation of our thinking.

Right now the Christian community is no longer a contender in the war of ideas. Because we are not at the gate, the church is hearing about ideas long after they have made it into the culture. Because of this, the church is forced to constantly react and play "defense" against the prevailing wind of culture. The church is forced into a cycle of relevance that demands adapting to trends birthed in an anti-christian environment.

Sadly, there are very few new ideas being birthed in that environment. I have coined a word to describe what I see happening: *discreativity.*

We are seeing discreativity manifesting itself in many arenas. For example, recently I was sent a series of photographs of Detroit, Michigan. Detroit recently filed bankruptcy, and the photos were of modern ruins of what had been the wealthiest city in the United States. Because of many decisions that rejected new creative ideas, the city has become a living example of discreativity. This same situation is happening in the realm of education and the arts. The most glaring display of discreativity is seen in the film industry and television. Rather than creating something that is really new, good, or beautiful; the modern world is often putting out remakes of old stories. To cover up the lack of freshness, gratuitous sex or explosions are thrown in to titillate the viewer. The end product is actually destructive in nature—it is *discreative.*

Because the church has stepped back from the gate, the church and the culture have suffered. The world is not hearing anything fresh and restorative, and the church is forced to mimic rather than influence culture. But Jesus said we are the salt of the earth. In other words, we give preservation and flavor to the world around us. Because we have access to heaven we can bring life to our fallen world.

The place at the gate is the battle ground where the warrior artist needs to fight.

This is a scary place for many, because it requires excellence in your craft, and a deep grounding in your faith.

Recently a gifted musician in my church entered a contest to rewrite the Folger's coffee jingle. Her name is Courtney Reid and she won the contest. She was given a trip to New York City, a nice cash prize, and some time with insiders in the music industry. That is a cool story. What's even cooler is that Courtney sings in a local bar on Saturday nights. Sometimes she sings prophetically over the people in the bar, and people come to hear her because something about her and her group is different. Courtney has chosen to take a place at the gate in her community.

Another gifted friend of mine, Julie Lavender, has taken her home in New Hampshire and turned it into a recording studio. She has created a radio program called *Dream Farm* that is beginning to get traction on public radio stations and is attracting world class jazz musicians as guests. Julie is using her platform to impact these men and women with her life and witness as a Messianic believer. Julie recently finished a recording called the *Siddur Project* that set the Hebrew Prayer Book to modern jazz. Because of the high quality of the music, Julie was able to attract musicians who were not believers to participate in the project.

Not long ago I met a young woman who recently graduated from college, and she wanted to meet with me because she felt God was calling her to start a Christian theater company. She wanted to impact the community with Christian drama, and she also wanted to raise money for the poor and needy through theater that reflected her values. All of that was wonderful.

Then she told me how she was planning on moving to Minnesota to be part of a small Christian theatre company.

I challenged her to reconsider, and to go to New York for a season and learn her craft. I knew that if she really wanted her vision to be successful, she would need to develop skills and a level of excellence that could only be learned in a major theatrical center like New York. She walked away from our conversation discouraged and disappointed. She admitted (and I agreed) New York is a scary place. I'm not sure if she was prepared for me to challenge her or push her out of her comfort zone.

We are in a war, and the church can no longer bless or encourage second rate "Christian" art–whether it be theater, a "Christian" pop-rock band, or another second rate "Christian" pulp fiction writer. The world is crying out for men and women with the guts to learn their craft and be better than their counterparts in the "secular" arena. God is looking for someone who is willing to be the foolish one who confounds the wise.

THE DIFFICULT PATH

Taking a seat at the gate is not an easy choice. It requires knowing your craft and being as good as, or better than, your contemporaries. It requires not copying the tired trends of the world. It requires keeping fresh, setting trends rather than following them, and having a prophetic vision for where things might be headed down the road. You will need to sparkle with the energy of heaven. You will need to be grounded firmly in your faith, knowing that you really do have the answers to the questions people are asking. And if you don't, you will have to depend on God to give you the word that is needed at that moment.

This is a high calling. Are you ready to hone your craft and know your story in order to release the sound and vision of heaven in the gate of your arena of influence?

I know of another musician who struggled with becoming excellent at his craft. He struggled for years carrying a heavy load as the head worship leader at his church. Often his pay was sub-standard and the demands on him were heavy. Each week he was required to compose new songs for his worship team to sing. He was a gifted musician, but was not appreciated during his lifetime. This happened partly because he made what he did look easy. One hundred years after his death people began studying the manuscripts that he left behind. They were stunned to read in the margins of the musical pages "Jesus helped me here." At the end of every musical score he wrote in latin, "to the Glory of God alone." The man was J.S. Bach. When I was studying music theory, often the teacher would remark, "Bach did it." In nearly 300 years it turns out there hasn't been one new musical idea that J.S. Bach didn't first explore.

Bach took a seat at the gate, but he did something greater than that, he left a legacy for those who followed after him.

TO RECAP:
- Although Christians still command an extraordinary majority in the United States, many feel they are a persecuted minority.
- The place at the gate will give you influence in the moment you need it.
- The place at the gate is the battle ground where the warrior artist needs to fight.
- We are in a war, and the church can no longer bless or encourage second rate "Christian" art.
- Taking a seat at the gate requires knowing your craft and being as good as, or better than, your contemporaries.

CHAPTER SEVENTEEN

LIVING FOR THE NEXT GENERATION

When I directed a pregnancy resource center, I had this quote from Psalm 78 on my office wall:

> *He established a testimony in Jacob, and appointed a law in Israel,which he commanded to our fathers to teach to their children; That the next generation might know them, the children yet unborn, so that they might set their hope in God, and not forget the works of God, but keep his commandments. (Psalm 78:5-7)*

At this moment, the moment of the story, there may be no greater calling than this one–to live for those who have not even been born. We have no idea how important our legacy is. Every choice we make can impact generations to come after us.

A LONG LEGACY

In the mid-1600's a wave of immigration came out of England to the new Massachusetts colony. This "Great Migration" was driven by men and women looking to escape the religious oppression in England and the English Civil War. There was a deep desire to form a new colony formed on a relationship with God. In each of the early towns of New England, these men and women made covenants with God that were left as testimonies to those in the future.

This early vision for the government of God in North America was ended abruptly by two events. In the 1660's a local native American chief started an uprising that resulted in the burning of villages and the destruction of mission work among the "Praying Indians." A puritan pastor was having great success leading the native peoples to Christ, and then forming establishing settlements of these new converts. "King Philip's War," as it came to be known, began the long history of bloodshed and broken promises between the Europeans and the Native people. It also resulted in the near extinction of the Praying Indians.

In 1692 another event occurred that permanently altered the future of New England. In a settlement west of Salem, Massachusetts four teenage girls began playing with a slave from the West Indies. This slave, named Tituba, was a priestess in West African religion, and was exposing the girls to what we now call Voodoo. As their dabbling in the occult became more involved, each of the "circle girls" began to have frightening experiences, and with the guidance of Tituba, began to accuse men and women in the community of witchcraft. At the time witchcraft was a capital offense under English law. Before the summer of 1692 was over, 18 innocent people were executed. Most of them were leaders in the church and community.

In 1706, Anna Putnam, the leader of the circle girls, publicly repented. A generation later Jonathan Edwards stated that this confession began the First Great Awakening.

Today I live in Salem, Massachusetts. Many of the events I have shared happened to my ancestors, and I do ministry on the plot of land that belonged to one of my great-grandfathers. Every day I am confronted with the evidence of decisions made by men and women over 300 years ago.

We have no idea how we are impacting future generations.

Albert Outler wrote in the preface to John Wesley's sermons that the Methodist revival was actually greater in the second generation than the first.[14] I think we are seeing a similar thing happening in regards to the charismatic movement that began in the 1960's. We are now 50 years later, and that movement has been reignited by successive waves of the Holy Spirit and impacting nations across the globe.

BIGGER THAN YOUR DESTINY

For the past 8 years much of my ministry has been helping men and women find their true calling. I read a lot about helping men and women find the right career path. Ultimately, I want to see men and women walk into their destiny. I want to see people do the thing that burns inside of them. I believe that they will be happier, and that the world will be a better place because people are being who they are meant to be.

Even so, having your own destiny fulfilled is not enough. It's not about you, and your needs. Being a part of the Army Arising, bearing the Person, Presence, and Power of God requires that you walk into your destiny not just for you but for those who come after you. You need to fulfill your destiny for the sake of the destinies of those you may never know.

I lived in Florida for a few years, and one of the common bumper stickers I saw read "I am spending my children's inheritance."

---

14 Wesley, John, and Albert Cook Outler. *The Works of John Wesley.* Nashville: Abingdon Press, 1984, page 1.

That seems funny at first, but Proverbs 13:22 tells us, "A good man leaves an inheritance to his *children's children,* but the sinner's wealth is laid up for the righteous (emphasis mine)." People who live thinking that they can use all that they have in this life for themselves are truly evil, not good. The idea that you get all you can in this life and leave your children to pay the bills is the opposite of God's plan for you and for the world. Any philosophy or culture that puts the comfort and pleasure of an older generation ahead of the life, health, or nurture of the next generation is a culture of death.

WORKING FOR LABAN

When I first entered ministry an older man told me to find the person that I wanted to be like and "carry his bags." Essentially, serve and become a son to a father in the Lord. God always raises up men and women of God who are first sons and daughters to other Fathers and Mothers in the faith. Sadly, I came of age in a time when most of the leaders before me were "spending their children's inheritance." They saw in me talent, and sought to use my gifts to build their ministries. This was similar to the situation Jacob found himself in when he worked for Laban. Laban made promises to Jacob that he never intended to keep. Jacob worked for Laban 14 years before he finally left, with most of Laban's wealth and family (Genesis 29-31).

I also did this for 14 years, and called these the "Laban years." Eventually I had to choose to let God be my Father. I also walked through a long process of forgiving the fathers before me who chose not to be fathers. Most importantly, I chose to be a father to those who follow me. I have made it a principle to give to the younger men and women guidance to avoid some of my mistakes.

I guess to sum it up–it's not about me and my ministry. I work for my Father. I am privileged to share in His family business. The goal is to train and equip others to continue the family business successfully after I'm gone.

HEALING RELATIONSHIPS

If you are going to be in the Army Arising, you need to embrace the ultimate call to being a son who becomes a father. The last prophet in the Old Testament ended his book by looking forward to the return of Elijah the prophet who will "turn the hearts of the fathers to the children and the hearts of the children to the fathers" (Malachi 4:6).

The Army Arising isn't about perpetuating the cult of youth that has pervaded the church, or about making sure that you get your ministry, career or brand established. This army is about re-establishing intergenerational relationships, establishing the healthy family of God in the earth.

You might be feeling a little angry and anxious about what I have said. You may have been abused, neglected or hurt by your earthly father, or your fathers in the faith. This is a reality, and why so many have called this the "fatherless generation." Like Nicodemus you probably are saying "I can't climb back into my mother's womb and be born again!" (John3:4) You can't go back in time and be "refathered." I frequently meet men and women who are looking for someone to mentor them, or for someone to be the father they never had. I have learned that any effort to get your need met in another person will be a failure.

---

15 When the Bible discusses being a "son" this is not sexist language, but rather a statement of rights. In the ancient world a son had the rights to inheritance, property and privilege that daughters did not have. Whether you are a man or woman, you have all the rights that a first born son had in that world.

But there is hope! Through the Holy Spirit you can experience healing, wholeness, and the assurance that you are God's son[15]--and if a son, an heir. You have an inheritance. If you have an inheritance, then you have one to pass on as well. You get to steward your niche in the "family business", as it were, and make sure it prospers in your generation. Then you get to teach the upcoming generation how to find their niches and begin to prosper in their generation.

And there is healing for the father wound. As my book *The Glory of a Wasted Life* recounts, my life is living proof that God can and will heal you and help you walk into wholeness. If there is any chapter in the Bible that lays out the keys to this healing, it is Romans chapter 8. I return to it often.

GETTING HEALED

Leanne Payne once wrote in *Restoring the Christian Soul Through Healing Prayer* that there are three obstacles to healing: failure to forgive others, failure to forgive one's self, and the failure to come into self-acceptance.[16] In order to live for the next generation we need to forgive the parents and leaders in our lives who have hurt, neglected, or abused us. We need to let go of our right to seek revenge for the sins of the fathers.

Next, we need to forgive ourselves for our sinful reaction to the sins of the previous generation. Rebellion and resisting authority are sins; they are not being "prophetic," or being "a pioneer." A knee-jerk reaction to instructions and rules, or to coming under authority, are warning signs that you need to seek God, ask forgiveness, and be forgiven before you can fully embrace sonship.

16 Payne, Leanne, and Leanne Payne. *Restoring the Christian Soul Through Healing Prayer: Overcoming the Three Great Barriers to Personal and Spiritual Completion in Christ.* Wheaton, Ill: Crossway Books, 1991.

After forgiving comes letting go. Self-acceptance is coming to the place where you know that only God can make things right. You cannot "try harder" to undo the sins of the past. It means accepting the things you cannot change, and accepting means letting go of control. Most of the people who have deep father wounds also have a deep need to be in control. But as long as you hold on to control, God cannot be in control.

Finally, you need personal prayer for healing. If you follow these steps, you will begin to see God heal you. This is not an easy process, and I believe that is why often people forgive but still feel pain. After you forgive you need to ask God to heal the broken place in your heart that causes your pain.

In other words, forgiving others, forgiving yourself, and coming into self acceptance are the prerequisites for healing. They do not heal in themselves. God does the healing, you have to put your faith in him. Once again, you cannot do it alone. You need help.

I can attest from my own experience, the pain will go away.

When we come into the healing of this generational brokenness creativity is released in a new level. Ideas will flow freely, and you will become more free to give to others–not to meet your need for acceptance and significance–but to bless, honor, and encourage others.

God wants you to leave a legacy. Your creative call can impact generations to come, and change history. And this process of honoring and supporting following generations will be the process that leads us to our final destination–the city built by the Master Artisan himself.

Let's close this chapter with a "first step" prayer toward generational healing:

Father, we thank you that you want us to be members of your family who give life to the world. This is a broken place, and I have been hurt by the failure of the fathers and mothers in my life. I choose to forgive those who have hurt, neglected, or abandoned me and left me to find my own way in the world without their love and guidance. I choose to forgive them now in Jesus' name.

(Take a few moments to forgive and release any specific things God may bring to mind.)

I also ask forgiveness now for my sinful reaction to the sins of the fathers and mothers in my life. Forgive me for resisting authority, rebelling against the order you have given us, and choosing to reject parts of Your nature and ways that you created. Rebellion is as the sin of witchcraft, and any area where I have allowed demonic torment through rebellion I now confess. I also ask you to forgive me for believing the lie that You, Father, are like my earthly parents. Forgive me for believing that you are not a good Father. Forgive me now in Jesus' name.

I choose to embrace all that you have created for me. Heal the hurts of the past, and restore to me anything that generational sin has stolen from me. Any areas where I have not been free to give you, I

*now ask you to heal. Help me live for those who are
yet to be born, and help me to be a good father or
mother to the next generation. All this I ask through
your Son Jesus Christ. Amen.*

TO RECAP:
- We do not know how much we will impact following generations.
- God's plan is for fathers to leave a legacy for sons.
- God can heal generational brokenness.
- The obstacles to healing are the failure to forgive others, the failure to forgive one's self, and the failure to come into self-acceptance.
- God wants you to leave a legacy.

CHAPTER EIGHTEEN

LOOKING FOR A CITY

In Hebrews 11:10 we are told that Abraham and the others who lived by faith were "looking for a city that has foundations whose architect and builder is God." As you may remember from the beginning of this book, "architect and builder" is a translation of the Hebrew word "charash." Charash is the warrior artisan described in Zechariah 1:9. We have come full circle as we come to the end of the book.

Why did God call you to join the army of artists? Was it to have a career doing what you love? Was it to give you an opportunity to release your prophetic gift through creativity? Was it to preach the gospel in an unconventional way?

Although all of these reasons for entering the army of artists are valid, there is only one reason. It is the same reason Abraham left the land of the Chaldeans, Moses left Egypt, and my ancestors left England for a strange new world. They were looking for a city not made with hands, whose Architect and Builder is God.

God is looking for men and women who will make a way for the coming of the Lord.

This is a unique moment in time, the moment of the story, and the moment when we can begin to almost hear creation groan. There is a longing in the whole created order for the revealing of the sons and daughters of God and for the return of the rightful King who will put all things in order.

A BIGGER STORY

So many of the men and women with whom I spend time are so caught in the cycle of survival that they begin to forget that there is a bigger story happening today. History and time seem to be speeding up in anticipation of the great and glorious day of the Lord.

When I first became a Christian, it was an assumed belief that the church would be getting less and less influential as the world became darker and darker. At this dark moment the rapture would happen and the seven year Great Tribulation would occur. Then Jesus would come back and judge the earth and burn it up. Then we could come back and live in the New Heaven and New Earth. The numbers of books and sermons I have heard unpacking how and when this would happen is astounding. One pastor I remember even gleefully looked forward to watching the tribulation from a cloud in heaven.

I was astounded to learn that this interpretation of the future is actually pretty recent. It emerged in the 1840's, and didn't even get a strong following until the 1920's. Before then Christians believed that Jesus was coming back to a glorious church that had transformed the world and prepared for him to return. Yes, there would be injustices to put into order, but the plan seemed to be that our job was to make life "on earth as it is in heaven."

Charles Wesley's vision of the return of Jesus is triumphant, not tribulating:

> *Lo! He comes with clouds descending,*
> *Once for favored sinners slain:*
> *Thousand, thousand saints attending*
> *Swell the triumph of His train;*
> *Hallelujah! Hallelujah!*
> *God appears on earth to reign.*
>
> *Every eye shall now behold Him,*
> *Robed in dreadful majesty;*
> *Those who set at naught and sold Him,*
> *Pierced and nailed Him to the tree,*
> *Deeply wailing, deeply wailing*
> *Shall the true Messiah see.*
>
> *The dear tokens of His passion*
> *Still His dazzling body bears;*
> *Cause of endless exultation*
> *To His ransomed worshippers;*
> *With what rapture, with what rapture,*
> *Gaze we on those glorious scars!*
>
> *Yea, Amen! Let all adore Thee,*
> *High on Thy eternal throne;*
> *Savior, take the power and glory,*
> *Claim the kingdom for Thine own;*
> *Hallelujah! Hallelujah!*
> *Everlasting God come down!*

Imagine the day when the saints on earth join the saints in heaven in proclaiming "The kingdoms of this world have become the Kingdom of our Lord and of his Christ!" This vision of a triumphant Jesus returning to claim the kingdom for his own moved our ancestors to found schools, hospitals, and orphanages. It moved them to end slavery, end child labor, and promote temperance. They believed in a call to "build Jerusalem in every green and pleasant land."

Recently I have noticed a trend away from the rapture vision of the future to the vision of Jesus coming to reign on the earth. This other vision, expecting to reign with Jesus as kings and priests on the earth, is why God is raising up an army of artists called to build Jesus Christ a throne in the earth.

A DIFFERENT VISION

One night I dreamed a dream that surprised me. I saw Jerusalem, and I was standing on the Temple Mount. The Dome of the Rock was no longer there, but there were no buildings. It seemed as though there was a tent or a pavilion on the Mount. I also saw beautiful banners and flags that fluttered in the wind. It was late in the day and the pale pink of sunset was beginning to appear in the sky. There were musicians, and dancers. In the center of this pageant there were reporters and film crews from international news networks filming the event. At the center of the entire scene was Jesus, sitting on his throne, reigning from Jerusalem. On his head he wore a glorious crown of thorns, transformed from an instrument of torture to an emblem of triumph. All of this was live, and the world was watching as a healed and restored Army of Artists worshiped Jesus on his throne in Jerusalem.

This is not a book about eschatology (the study of the end times). It is a book for those of us called to live in the end times, called to prepare for the day when all will be made right, when Jerusalem shall be called holy, and all nations will come to worship Jesus on the holy mountain.

That's a pretty big vision, and little bit bigger than painting prophetic paintings in front of a church.

This is a moment in time when ideas have power, and ideas are most powerfully transferred through story, through song, through film, and through media. You have made it through this book, and made it to this question: Are you going to get a vision for this moment when we have the opportunity to shape human history and prepare the way for the coming of the Lord? Are you looking for the city?

EXTRAORDINARY TIMES

Seven years ago when I left my job and began living by faith I was gripped by fear. I was afraid of rejection, and afraid of failure. All of those fears made sense when I thought that we were living in ordinary times. The truth is, we are not living in ordinary times, but extraordinary times. There is an old Chinese curse that goes: "May you live in interesting times." If nothing else, our twenty-first century world is interesting.

Throughout this book I have asked the same question in various ways. Will you say "yes" to God, and be used by Him? Will you make the choice to live for His glory alone? Will you come to Him, as broken and mixed up as you are and surrender yourself as a living sacrifice? Will you give God your intellect, your creativity, your career plan, and even your gifts and say "let it be to me according to your word?"

If you can say "yes" to these questions, you are a warrior artist. You are becoming part of that army Jesus has called to prepare the way for his return. You are the one called to shape ideas, soften hearts, and preach the gospel at all times. You are the one to get a revelation of heaven and share that revelation through the work of your hands. You are a world changer, a culture shifter and an idea shaper.

You are God's secret weapon for this moment in time, the moment of the story. You are the artisan who is crafting something that strikes terror in those who terrorize God's people. This is your moment to shine. This is your moment to rise.

You are called to be a means of grace and a living sacrament for this world. You are called to say, "Fear not!"

Because you believe, you are born to do the impossible. You are called to build a throne for Jesus on the earth. You are called to make history, not just live in it. Because Jesus lives in you, everyone you meet will meet Jesus in you. You and the gifts that are expressed through you will begin to shape and transform the world around you.

You are blessed to be called to this moment, this army, this vision, this City. You are blessed to be made in the Image of the Invisible God, the Master Artisan of the City not made with hands. You are God's masterpiece, shaped and fashioned to be a secret weapon for this end-time army of artists.

Bring me my bow of burning gold!
Bring me my arrows of desire!
Bring me my spear! O clouds, unfold!
Bring me my chariot of fire!
I will not cease from mental fight,
Nor shall my sword sleep in my hand,
Till we have built Jerusalem
In [every] green and pleasant land. [17]

17 Blake, William, From the prologue to *Milton,* alt. 90

POSTSCRIPT

In I Chronicles 17 David has a conversation with God. David tells God that he wants to build Him a house to replace the tent that was used for worship. In response, God spoke to David and told him not to build a house of worship. Instead, God promised that He would build David a house.

This is the Davidic Covenant, that there would be an everlasting King on the throne of David.

About eight years ago I sensed the Lord telling me to pray for a house. This was about a year before I began doing the work I am doing today. I believe it was out of those initial prayers for a house that God birthed the work that was the inspiration for this book.

When the Lord gave me a clear call to "raise up an army of artists who build Jesus a throne in the earth" I was praying daily for a house. I imagined some small house that would be my base of operations. Eventually the "ministry" I was doing needed a name. I was deeply impacted by the late Ingrid Trobisch and her teaching on the concept of "geborgenheit." This is a German word that describes the sense of protection, safety, and being established that many artists rarely find. Although I loved the concept, I already had one strange German name to explain, so I kept looking for inspiration. This is when I turned to a book of poetry by David

Whyte that also communicated the ideas taught by Ingrid Trobisch. David Whyte's book, The House of Belonging, has traveled with me for many years, and it seemed like an obvious place to look for inspiration.

Mr. Whyte, and his publisher, Many Rivers Press, graciously gave me permission to use the name Belonging House. Through a lot of twists and turns the name has stayed.

Well, back to the house. So we (by that point I had a small band of fellow adventurers) began praying for a house, and we eventually set our sights on a mansion in Akron, Ohio as a center for art, teaching, prayer, and creating geborgenheit.

God is a God of surprises. This house has become a lot of one on one conversations over coffee, and many hours of worship and prayer in two crisis pregnancy centers, a Spanish speaking church in the South End of Boston, and in an historic church in Salem, Massachusetts. The house is the group of men and women who read a weekly email update that I write. The house is the men and women who read my blog, and send me amazing testimonies from around the world about the call God has given them to be a world changer through their art.

Still the need for dedicated space has always been part of the vision of Belonging House. A permanent home would meet four needs:

Being—Belonging House is called to host the Presence of God and be an embassy of heaven. Part of our house will be designated space for prayer, worship, and listening to God. We need a prayer room.

Becoming—Belonging House is called to train, equip, and heal, men and women with a creative call. Part of the house will have space for "hands on workshops," training seminars, and inner healing ministry. We need teaching space and office space.

Belonging—Belonging House is a place where artistic men and women can find rest, be understood, and have community. We need a house for a gathering space to share meals, hold small gatherings, celebrations, and provide hospitality for guests and small retreats. We need a kitchen, bedrooms, and a dining area.

Building—Belonging House is about raising up others who build the kingdom of God, prepare for the return of Jesus, and create the culture of heaven through creativity. What happens beyond the house is more important than the house itself, as this center impacts the world. We need a connection to media and the internet to share what we do outside the house.

We are looking for the "hub" that will make all of this possible. A designated home for being, becoming, belonging, and building. We are looking for a home for Belonging House.

Yes, I believe one day we will have a house. But, like God's promise to David, I know that a house might look very different than a building with four walls and wood paneling. David's house has become a house containing every tribe, language, people, and nation.

The challenge we all face is not having a God sized vision. His ways are not our ways, and the things that we see as limitations God often views as opportunities. I hope that this book has stirred up a God-sized vision for your life and your craft.

If this book has blessed you, or if you want to learn more about Belonging House and how you can really be a part of the army arising, send me an email at
AnArmyArising@belonginghouse.org.

WORKS CITED

Eikleberry, Carol. *The Career Guide for Creative and Unconventional People*. Berkeley, Calif: Ten Speed Press, 2007.

Elsheimer, Janice. *The Creative Call: An Artist's Response to the Way of the Spirit*. Colorado Springs, Colo: Shaw Books, 2001.

Merton, Thomas. *New Seeds of Contemplation*. New York, NY: New Directions, 1972.

Payne, Leanne, and Leanne Payne. *Restoring the Christian Soul Through Healing Prayer: Overcoming the Three Great Barriers to Personal and Spiritual Completion in Christ*. Wheaton, Ill: Crossway Books, 1991.

Tommey, Matt. *Unlocking the Heart of the Artist*. [S.l.]: The Worship Studio, 2010.

Wesley, John, and Albert Cook Outler. *The Works of John Wesley*. Nashville: Abingdon Press, 1984.

Whyte, David. *The House of Belonging*: Poems. Langley, Wash: Many Rivers Press, 1997.

Made in the USA
Lexington, KY
09 February 2014